JEWISH THINKERS

General Editor: Arthur Hertzberg

Buber

Forthcoming titles in the series

BIALIK
David Aberbach

RASHI
Chaim Pearl

HEINE
Ritchie Robertson

MENDELSSOHN
Arthur Hertzberg

ARLOSOROFF
Shlomo Avineri

BEN-GURION
Eli Shaltiel

WEIZMANN
Arthur Hertzberg

JUDAH HALEVI
David Goldstein

BA'AL SHEM TOV AND THE HASIDIC MOVEMENT
Ada Rapoport-Albert

IBN GABIROL
Raphael Loewe

AHAD HA'AM
Steven Zipperstein

MAIMONIDES
Amos Funkenstein

Buber

Pamela Vermes

PETER HALBAN

WEIDENFELD & NICOLSON

LONDON

FIRST PUBLISHED IN GREAT BRITAIN BY
PETER HALBAN PUBLISHERS LTD
42 South Molton Street
London W1Y 1HB
1988

British Library Cataloguing in Publication Data

Vermes, Pamela
Buber.——(Jewish thinkers series).
1. Buber, Martin
I. Title II. Series
193 B3213.B84

ISBN 1-87001-507-X

Typeset at Oxford University Computing Service
Printed in Great Britain by
Butler & Tanner Ltd, Frome, Somerset

CONTENTS

Note on Transliteration

The general system of transliteration has been used. The dot under the H has been included to denote the Hebrew letter *chet* and has been used where essential to pronunciation or meaning. An inverted comma has been used to denote the Hebrew letters *aleph* and *eyin*, e.g. Ba'al.

Acknowledgements

Acknowledgement is due to Verlag Lambert Schneider for permission to quote from *Briefwechsel aus Martin Buber: sieben Jahrzehnten.* Band III: 1938–1965

Acknowledgement is also made to Kösel Verlag for permission to quote from *Werke I, Schriften zur Philosophie* by Martin Buber.

INTRODUCTION

More than two thousand people crammed into every available space of the Park Avenue synagogue in New York on 13 July 1965, one month after Martin Buber's death, to take part in the memorial service and to hear the addresses relayed over loudspeakers. 'This puts to rest, more effectively. than words can do,' Werner Cahnman wrote afterwards in *The Reconstructionist*, 'the whispering campaign that had been carried on for years, that Martin Buber was an esoteric philosopher whom hardly anybody could understand and whose quality as a genuine interpreter of Jewish values was dubious.'[1]

Who was he then, this gifted man who throughout a long life managed to range with ease from philosophy to education, to psychology, to politics, to biblical studies and further? He himself emphatically refused to accept that he was a philosopher at all. He was not, he said, interested in ideas in themselves, but only in communicating his personal experience to others. If he used the language and methods of philosophy, it was because he knew of no other way to express as applicable to everyone the insights he had gained as an individual.

He similarly rejected the suggestion that he was a theologian. His name appears in the company of others such as Tillich, Bonhoeffer and Bultmann, but he always made it more than clear that he felt himself unqualified to pronounce on God's essential nature. He could only write about him in his relation with man. 'I cannot,' he wrote, 'forget that man lives face to face with God, but I also cannot at any point draw God himself into my explanation,

> any more than I can detach what is to me the undoubted effect of God in history and make it the object of my

consideration. Just as I know of no theological world-history, so I know of no theological anthropology in this sense. I know only of a philosophical one.

The theological element that has admittedly determined a great part of my study and writing is the basis of my thinking, but not as deriving from something traditional, however important this is to me too, and therefore not as 'theology', but rather as the religious experience to which I am indebted for the independence of my thought.[2]

Was Buber a mystic? Many think so. He undeniably passed through a phase in which mysticism was deeply attractive to him. His doctoral thesis was written on 'The history of the problem of individuation: Nicholas of Cusa and Jacob Boehme', and in 1909 he published an anthology of writings by ecstatics, mostly Christian.[3] Besides, a strong mystical thread runs through his rendering of Hasidic teachings and stories. Nevertheless, he came to believe that mysticism is 'unreal' according to his understanding of the word 'real', and he refused to accept the feasibility of the declared aim of the mystic, union with God. Where there is true relation, there can be no swallowing up of an *I* by a *You*; the two must always remain distinct. By the time he composed *I and Thou*, he had therefore abandoned the 'mystical bombast' of which his friend Franz Rosenzweig complained, and was writing instead of the indivisibility of the sacred and the profane and of the pointlessness of seeking God by leaving the world.

Another question which may reasonably be asked is whether Buber was basically a teacher. This would seem difficult to contradict. Yet he wished to make sure that his role was interpreted as that of a guide rather than an instructor. 'I demonstrate reality,' he insisted. 'I demonstrate something in reality that is no longer seen, or seen too little. I take my listener by the hand and lead him to the window. I push open the window and point outward. I have no doctrine. I conduct a conversation.'[4] His intention was to indicate a path to follow, not to explain in detail how to reach a destination.

I certainly do not hand a book of principles to someone who accepts my pointer, where he can see how to decide in any given situation. That is not for me. One whose finger is outstretched has one thing to show, not a variety. No, I have in fact no ethical system to offer. Neither do I know of any that is generally applicable and that I should only need to teach.[5]

Was Buber then a biblical scholar? Here the answer must be that despite the forty years or so spent in the study of Scripture, present-day specialists do not accept him as one of themselves. The reason they give is that where a detached analysis of biblical sources and language is required, Buber aimed primarily at an existential understanding of the text, and thought cold critical methods by themselves to be inadequate for such a task. He used them, but for him the Bible was first and foremost the record of a dialogue between heaven and earth, a living word which must be allowed to make its own living impact.

At least there can be no doubt that Buber was a Zionist. But even here, he belonged to a minority which struggled for a compromise with the Palestinian Arabs, abhorred bloodshed, and looked for a shared and peaceful occupation and government of the land of Israel.

Can he have been a *hasid*? After all, one whole volume of his collected works is entitled Hasidic Writings. The reply must be: most definitely not. No *hasid* would accept the indifference towards religious observances which Buber preached and explicitly practised. Indeed, while describing himself as an 'arch-Jew', he made no secret of his mistrust and even dislike of institutional religion. In a BBC interview with John Freeman on 14 December 1961, he declared himself very glad that the word 'religion' is not to be found in the Bible. In effect, while not actually proclaiming *nulla salus* nisi *extra ecclesiam*, no salvation *unless* outside the church, he made it clear in the work of his youth, maturity and old age that he regarded the life of the spirit to be threatened rather than fostered by adherence to a formalized religious cult of any persuasion. His primary objection was to religion's intrinsic nature. It was intolerable to him that it should set itself apart as a sacred speciality, with a code and regimen centred on God in rather the same way that a businessman's is centred on trade. He called instead for true religiousness, for the recognition of divine Presence in everyday life, for a watching and listening for what is being asked, and for an answering by means of deeds done in a spirit of love and obedience. Religion that is real, he writes in *Eclipse of God*, or desires to be real, will work for its own obliteration. From being a preoccupation with particular religious activities, it will seek redemption from the specific, wishing God so to enter the whole of business on earth that all of it will become sacrament, all of it temple, all of it priesthood. Confessing itself to be God's exile, religion will look for his Kingdom not beyond the grave but in the here and now, in human life 'lived without arbitrariness before the face of God'. As Paul Tillich said on the occasion of the memorial service, Buber 'anticipated freedom from religion, including the institutions of religion, in the name of that towards which religion points'. This may in part explain his appeal to the contemporary secular world for which, in a time of God's eclipse, the traditional assertions of churches and synagogues have become largely irrelevant.

When his works come to be considered, the following main themes will be seen to emerge. Buber asks for a return to relation in every field of life. Where the Hebrew prophets preach a turning back to God, in Hebrew *teshuvah*, Buber's summons is to a turning back, not to a continuous stand of relation, which would be impossible to sustain, but to a state of constant readiness for relation vis-à-vis life in this world, and a turning back *thereby* to relation with an Absolute Vis-à-Vis both in and out of this world. He hopes for an imitation of the attributes of a Supreme Vis-à-Vis whom, as will appear, he envisages in a very special way. And he asks of the individual and society that it will, by that means, hasten the coming of the Kingdom of God on earth.

Buber was in short, and by his own definition, a Hebrew thinker and a *Schriftsteller*, a writer.[6] But a straight translation is no use here because *Schriftsteller* is a pun. He was also a 'Schrift-Steller' that is to say, an exponent of Scripture, a writer who endeavoured to make the message of the Hebrew Bible accessible to the world of today.

Nor is this all, for he employs the closely related word 'Schriftstellerei', in connection with the writings of the Hasidim, the Jewish pietists who were to have such a deep influence on his thought. When he identified himself as a *Schriftsteller* he will also have had in mind the scriptures of Hasidism.

It was principally from these two sources, the Bible and Hasidism, that Buber, an existential interpreter, drew and reformulated truths which so many, Jews and non-Jews alike, have recognized as necessary to the development and wholeness of the human person.★

★ This brief account of Martin Buber's life and work relies often, especially in the summaries of his publications, on my earlier and much fuller study, *Buber on God and the Perfect Man*, 1980. All translations from Buber's works are my own.

I

FIRST INFLUENCES

Martin Buber wrote no autobiography. He left instead a collection of autobiographical fragments published very late in life but written at various periods.[1] Furthermore, even these few precious insights were designed to throw light not so much on himself as on the subject which gave the booklet its title and remained throughout one of the keys to his ideas: encounter, encounter as the high peak of relational life. Biographers writing since 1972 have nevertheless been fortunate in possessing three large volumes of correspondence to turn to. These letters, selected and introduced by Grete Schaeder[2] from among a mass of documents in the safekeeping of the Jewish National and University Library in Jerusalem, are of immense help in following Buber's movements, the climate of his thought, and his career in general. However, we still have nothing by way of intimate knowledge of him, or of his relations with those closest to him, apart from the occasional discreet exchange with his wife in the early years. Everything more personal has been omitted at the request of either his family or his surviving correspondents, but no doubt also because he did not himself care for disclosures concerning himself. As he wrote in 1951 in reply to a request for an autobiographical Foreword to a projected book: 'The thought that I should say, this is what I am, bothers me. I do not have that sort of relation to myself. Will you understand if I tell you that I take no interest in myself?'[3]

Buber was born in Vienna on 8 February 1878. For reasons so far unexplained, his parents' marriage soon broke up: his mother one day walked out of the house, leaving his father, Karl Buber, with the child aged three, and he did not see her again until he was himself a married man with children. Taken to live with his grandfather Salomon Buber and his wife Adele in their house in

Lemberg, then the capital of Austrian Galicia, he stayed with them until he was fourteen years old. (Strangely enough, he was in later years to take charge of his own grandchildren in exactly the same way when the marriage of his son Rafael failed.)

Penetrated by a sense of loss, the small boy waited impatiently but silently for his mother to return; she was never mentioned by his grandparents in his presence and he did not ask them about her. But one day, a year or so later, he was alone on the house balcony with an older girl deputed by his grandmother to take temporary charge of him, and she told him that his mother would never come back. The pain of that moment stayed with him throughout his childhood and beyond, but he accepted what the girl had said and ceased to wait for his mother's return from then on. He continued nevertheless to suffer from her absence and afterwards invented a word, *Vergegnung*, mis-encounter, to describe an encounter that should take place but does not. He said in his old age: 'I suspect that everything I experienced of genuine encounter during the course of my life had its origin in that moment on the balcony.'[4]

Apart from this sorrow, Martin's life as a young boy was comfortable and stimulating. Salomon Buber was a man of substance and learning, the owner of a phosphorus mine, a corn merchant, a banker, a leader of the Jewish community in Lemberg and a prominent member of the non-Jewish commercial fraternity, but also a dedicated scholar with a thorough knowledge of Hebrew, and a skilled editor of rabbinic works. Probably the boy saw little of him. It is in any case his grandmother Adele, and not her husband, who appears at the centre of another autobiographical fragment. Cultivated and very competent in business affairs—she took over much of her husband's responsibilities to leave him free to study and write— she exerted a lasting influence over her grandson, imbuing him with her own passion for German literature and for the spoken and written word. She taught him to use words accurately and in such a way that they needed no paraphrase, with the result that by the time he left her he had learnt 'what it meant to say something'. When his grandmother spoke to people, she 'really spoke' to them. His grandfather, he recalls, 'was a true philologist, a "lover of the word", but my grandmother's love for the genuine word influenced me even more strongly than his because that love was so direct and so devout.'[5]

Martin was educated at home, mainly in languages—Hebrew, Latin and French—until he was ten, and was then sent to the Polish Franz Josef gymnasium in Lemberg. Here, he says, the atmosphere was that which seemed to reign between the nations of the Austro-Hungarian monarchy, a sort of mutual sociability without mutual understanding. The children were mostly Poles (and instruction was in Polish), with a minority of Jews, and personally they got on well together. As groups, however, they hardly got to know each other at all. At the same time, Buber makes a point of attributing to the Poles no show of intolerance towards himself and other Jews, either from the teaching staff or the students. The only aspect of his school life that he hated was the morning assembly at 8 a.m. when a bell rang, a teacher took up his place beneath the great crucifix on the wall and, after making the sign of the cross, all began the morning prayers together. Until they could sit down again, Buber records, the Jewish children stood there 'with lowered eyes'. Although no effort was ever made to convert him, this regular experience of having to witness a ceremony which no part of him could share, filled him with a lasting aversion for missionary endeavours of all kinds, which even Franz Rosenzweig in later years was unable to overcome when he tried to win him over to a Jewish mission among non-Jews.

Karl Buber, who remarried, and with whom Martin went to live when he was fourteen years old, was another to leave on his son an enduring mark. Not outstanding except as a good farmer, and certainly no scholar—he observed once that his importance lay in being his father's son and his son's father—Karl was a kind and straightforward man concerned with the effectiveness of fertilizers and good breeding stock, and he impressed Martin with the attentive way in which he approached the people and even the animals around him and involved himself with their needs and cares. He would for instance greet his horses 'not just in a friendly way but really personally'.[6] His son says that he learned much from him that he had not found in books.

It was Karl Buber who was responsible for introducing the boy to a *zaddik*, the leader of the Hasidic community in a town called Sadgora in the province of Bukovina, near to where his father owned some land. The golden age of the saintly Hasidic teachers might have passed, and their spirituality might not have been what it was in the eighteenth and early nineteenth centuries, but Buber clearly remembered the 'shudder of awe' which gripped the community when the *rebbe* rose to speak. In his childish way, the boy concluded that this must be what life was all about. It had to do with the upright and just human being, with the helpful human person.

At fourteen, Buber's intellectual development was in full spate and, turning his back on the religion of his elders, a position he was to maintain for six years, he plunged with enthusiasm into his school work. Kant's *Prolegomena* soon made a great impact on him, easing his bewilderment about how to envisage time, either as having no beginning and no end, or as possessing both. The philosopher satisfied him with his proposition that time and space have no existence in themselves but are 'mere forms of sensory perception'. A few years later, when he was seventeen, his imagination was similarly gripped by Nietzsche's thesis that time is an everlasting return of the same thing, an endless sequence of endless continua resembling one another in every way, so that their final phases overflow into their beginnings. Although the young man could not accept this 'pseudo-mystery', it still temporarily, if negatively, seduced him.

By 1896, Buber was ready for higher studies and inscribed himself in the philosophical faculty of the University of Vienna, the city of his birth, but he attended lectures on such a wide variety of subjects—history of art, psychology, German studies, classical philology and even economics, not to mention his attendance at the psychiatric clinics—that he was clearly still unsure of what his path in life was to be. One of his chief excitements at this period was, however, associated with the theatre, to which he devotes another whole episode in *Meetings*. He visited the Burgtheater sometimes day after day, running up three flights of stairs after queuing for hours outside, and as he watched the dramatic piece unfolding below him, it was the word, the correctly spoken human word, that he absorbed into himself. 'Speech—it was only here, in this world of fiction out of fiction that it acquired its adequacy: certainly it appeared heightened, but to itself.'[7]

The third term of his university education was spent in Leipzig, where he celebrated his twentieth birthday. Later, he went on to Zurich, but it was in Leipzig that he came under the spell of Johann Sebastian Bach, who had been Cantor and later Court Composer in that city from 1723 to 1750. We are not told why Bach's music moved him so deeply, but he illustrates its effect on him by means of an anecdote. He had given a lecture on Ferdinand Lassalle, the German Jewish Socialist writer who founded the German Workers Union (which later evolved into the German Socialist Democratic Party), describing him as a hero after the model of Carlyle. Afterwards, he was congratulated on his performance and was at first gratified. Subsequently, however, he realized that the picture he had drawn was quite false. Disgusted with himself, he struggled for days to re-cast it. Of this experience he reports quite simply: 'Slowly, timidly and perseveringly, my insight grew into the reality of human existence and the difficulty of doing it justice. Bach helped me.'[8]

More importantly, it was at Leipzig also that Buber re-entered the Jewish world via Zionism, the movement recently founded by Theodor Herzl. He was still not sensitive to the religious aspect of Judaism. Zionism was for him mainly a vehicle for the renewal of Jewish culture and he devoted himself to the rediscovery of his inheritance, speaking and writing on Jewish topics—Jewish writers, Jewish painters, Jewish poets, Jewish folklore and legend, Jewish theatre, everything in fact that had to do with Jewish artistic creativity. The material that he and his friends assembled and published during those times now seems rather poor stuff, but it was the means by which the unsophisticated Jewishness of eastern Europe first became known to the intelligentsia of Austria and Germany.

In the winter of 1900, Buber established a section for art and knowledge in the Zionist Union in Berlin, whither he had moved for further study under Georg Simmel (1858–1918), the noted German sociologist and philosopher, and the philosopher

Wilhelm Dilthey (1833–1911), known for his development of an empathic understanding of history and life. 'Simmel and Dilthey were my teachers,' Buber wrote to Maurice Friedman in August 1951. 'In the years 1898–1904 they influenced my thought strongly, but to my knowledge had no influence at all on the I-you philosophy.'[9] At the invitation of Herzl, he took over the editorship of *Die Welt*, the official Zionist organ, from his friend Berthold Feiwel, spoke at meetings and composed pamphlets. He concerned himself exhaustively with all things Jewish and Zionist, including attending and addressing congresses. But he and his group had little in common with Herzl, who knew little and cared less about the Hebrew language or the artistic, spiritual and intellectual manifestations of Judaism. His one dream was to establish a homeland for the Jews: in fact, this was the time when the idea of settling them in East Africa came to be mooted.

Disagreement actually came into the open in 1901 with the formation of a splinter group in the Zionist movement known as the Democratic Fraction. Led by Leo Motzkin and Chaim Weizmann, this consisted largely of Russian Zionist students who demanded the separation of Zionism and religion, the organization of cultural activities, and the creation of a fund for the establishment of a Jewish university. The Fraction had initially much success against the political Zionism of Herzl and the co-founder of the World Zionist Organization, Max Nordau, but after a first representation at the Congress of 1901, a further consultation in 1904 saw only eleven people convening, among them Weizmann, Feiwel and Buber. Eventually, it petered out when it joined in the opposition to the East Africa scheme.

Meanwhile, however, a personal rift had erupted in 1903 between Buber, his friends and Theodor Herzl over the publication of the latter's novel, *Altneuland*.[10] A picture of Palestine, not as a Jewish state, but as a 'new society' in which Jews mingled peacefully and amicably with Arabs, and above all, in which immigrants from all over the world went about their business speaking the language of their former homelands instead of Hebrew, it attracted devastating criticism from Ahad Ha'am, one of the most influential thinkers of his generation and a major contributor to Hebrew literature.

Herzl's riposte was to summon to his aid his friend Nordau, who set about a free and vigorous attack on Ahad Ha'am in the Jewish press, with the result that Buber, Weizmann and Feiwel published a furious rejoinder by way of protest, signed by numerous supporters, in the Hebrew periodical *Ha-Zman* (The Time). Herzl took this as an act hostile to himself and to the Zionist movement, and despite Buber's several attempts by correspondence during most of May 1903 to mollify the Zionist leader, he did not succeed in his endeavour. No understanding existed between the two. Thus one of Herzl's final words of advice to the younger man was that he should try to find his way back to the Zionist movement (this apropos of his belonging to the Fraction), 'which certainly, like everything human, has its faults, but which I think for the most part consists of people of good will and in no way narrow-minded'.[11] Buber's reaction in a letter written the following day was dignified but determined, 'We do not need to find our way back to the movement since we stand as firm and upright in the movement as anyone else, and with all respect I cannot allow you to pronounce judgement on this.'[12]

When Herzl died the next year of heart disease (aged forty-four), Buber published at least two articles on him, one entitled simply 'Theodor Herzl',[13] the other 'Herzl and History'.[14] In them, he credited Herzl with exercising 'despite all the weaknesses' an immense influence on his surroundings and of possessing great charisma. But it was, he wrote, 'basically false to celebrate him as a *Jewish* personality. Nothing *elementarily* Jewish lived in Theodor Herzl'. The second of these pieces he ended thus: 'Living, building, erring, doing what is good and what is questionable for his people, he set up without knowing it a statue before the people to which the people gave his name. A statue without error and fault, with the pure traits of genius.'

Another fateful event of these years was Buber's marriage when he was twenty-one to Paula Winkler, a non-Jewish girl from Munich, who later made a reputation as a writer under the pseudonym of Georg Munk. From letters published in *Brief-wechsel* it is obvious that Buber depended on her in those days, and perhaps always, in more ways than one. Writing to her in a fit of depression, he told her: 'Your letters are the only thing. Besides them, perhaps the thought that there is a mother in you, the belief that there is . . . I have always and always looked for my mother.'[15] He turned to her also for practical help, getting her to knock into shape some of the rougher pieces of writing among his discoveries. Above all, she could be relied on to bring her husband down to earth whenever he threatened at that time to lose touch with reality.

Next to Paula, the most influential person in Buber's life at the turn of the century was the Socialist anarchist Gustav Landauer. Buber met him in Berlin in 1899 when Landauer was leading and teaching a group calling itself The New Community, whose aim was to anticipate a new era in art, beauty and religious dedication. Landauer, a Jew, spent many years preparing a fresh edition of Meister Eckhart's works, and was no doubt behind Buber's own involvement with mystical writings and his change of university studies from the history of art to Renaissance mysticism. But Landauer's political thought also had a great effect on Buber's own developing religious Socialism, and his awful end in the revolution in Germany which followed the First World War, when he was beaten and kicked to death in the street by soldiers in 1919, deeply distressed his friend.

In 1903–4 occurred what Buber might have called one of the 'little revelations' of his life. Suddenly, in the midst of all this activity, Zionist, scholarly and journalistic, he came across a document by the founder of Hasidism, the Ba'al Shem Tov (1700–60) and at once grasped, after all the years of indifference, the reality of the religiousness of Judaism, and specifically of its ancient belief that man is made in the image of God. This was the first of his most notable intuitions. (The second, which happened much later, concerned the nature of the divine model which, according to him, we are to imitate in order to become whole and truly human persons.) The story of his encounter with Hasidism must be told in his own words:

One day, I opened a little book entitled, *Zevaath Ribesh, The Testament of Rabbi Israel Ba'alshem*, and the words

8

flashed out at me: 'Let him thoroughly grasp the attribute of ardour. Let him rise ardently from his sleep for he is become holy and is another man and is worthy to beget,[16] and is become in accordance with the attribute of the Holy One, blessed be he, when he engendered worlds.'

It was then that, instantly overwhelmed, I came to understand the Hasidic soul. I discerned that most ancient of Jewish insights flowing in the darkness of exile into newly-conscious expression: man's likeness to God as deed, as development, as task. And this most Jewish notion was a most human one, the content of most human religiousness. It was then that I began to understand Judaism as religiousness, as piety, as *hasidut*. The image of my childhood, the memory of the *zaddik* and his community, arose and enlightened me. I perceived the idea of the perfect man. Immediately, I was aware of the call to proclaim it to the world.[17]

Shortly after this, Buber retired from active participation in Zionist work and gave himself over for five years to the study of Hasidism.

2

ENCOUNTER WITH HASIDISM

'Perfect', in Buber's vocabulary, does not mean without fault. When he wrote that he had 'perceived the idea of the perfect man', he did not intend to give the impression that he had found in Hasidism and its holy men sinless paragons, perfectly humble, perfectly charitable, perfectly good. He meant that he had found that by living in a certain way, the Hasidic teachers had managed to achieve and propagate an integrity which allowed a person to become all of one piece, to become perfectly human.

It should be made clear that certain scholarly objections have been raised against Buber's formulation of the movement founded by the Ba'al Shem Tov, the Master of the Good Name. His picture of its teachings and way of life does not correspond, it has been observed, to what emerges from the traditions handed down by the pupils of the Ba'al Shem and the legendary stories surrounding his name. Also, Buber's approach ignores the theoretical bases of Hasidism and depends almost exclusively on anecdotes and tales.[1] Buber's candid answer to this criticism was that he drew from Hasidism only what he felt was essential to it, and what he needed. He took from it only what he could pass on with benefit to others. He 'sieved' the material that he garnered. Indeed, he himself served as the 'sieve' in the same way as the prophets who, as he maintains in his biblical writings, served not merely as mouthpieces but took God's word into their hearts and reproduced it again from out of themselves so that it bore in addition their own mark upon it. Buber was presenting the 'scriptures' of eighteenth-century Hasidism as they were understood by him, a twentieth-century Jew. He laid emphasis on what he, from the perspective of another age, took to be truly Hasidic, and let fall whatever he discovered of superstition, magic and bigotry, of which there was also ample evidence and which he felt inappropriate to authentic religiousness.

Buber himself, as has been noted, rejected mysticism, arriving at the conclusion at an early stage of his development that its practice and teaching are in conflict with the fulfilment of the balanced human personality. He nevertheless belongs to Jewish mystical tradition. Tracing it backwards in time, his immediate source was the Polish-Russian Hasidism of the Ba'al Shem Tov, who inherited that of Kabbalah as it was interpreted in the sixteenth century by Isaac Luria Ashkenazi, which in turn evolved from medieval Kabbalah proper, which was preceded by what is known as Throne-Chariot mysticism and the parallel—though part of a very different stream—works of rabbinical literature going back to the early centuries of the Christian era, if not before. Medieval German Hasidism, which like Kabbalah adopted the Throne-Chariot vision as its main theme, also belongs to the same descent.

In reverse, and following very roughly the way forward from past to present, the speculations of the Throne-Chariot visionaries turned mainly on a text from chapters 1 and 10 of Ezekiel. The German *hasidim* and the Kabbalists took over these ideas, incorporated them into notions current in their own times and thereby generated a new body of thought. Later, Luria pioneered modifications to the very complex system of the Kabbalah. Meditating and teaching in the Levant more than a century before the Ba'al Shem, Luria greatly enriched Jewish ideas by popularizing notions until then closed to the ordinary person. The Ba'al Shem had been able to take this process further, giving meaning and direction not only to people with the time for lengthy reflection, but to the humble hard-working Jewish peasants, artisans, shop-keepers and inn-keepers of the towns and villages of eastern Europe.

Finally, this same body of doctrine and tradition was re-presented by Buber in such a way that it became comprehensible not only to the Jew, but to the larger non-Jewish world also. It was a sort of neo-Hasidism, one furthermore of which the classical Polish-Russian *hasid* might not have approved. A brief comparison of the progress envisaged in both would run more or less as follows. The Hasidic way begins with relation between man and God. For the sake of that relation, the spiritual path leads to a life of redemptive worship in the world. This in turn conduces to the fulfilment in man of the attributes accredited to God of unity and holiness, and thereby to the evolution of the unified human being and of the society and world of which he is part. Buber's way, set out in particular in *I and Thou*, turns the Hasidic process on its head. It starts with the development of relation between the individual and the people, creatures and things around him. It moves on *by this means* to the unification and realization of the person. And it ends with the growth of the ability to enter into what Buber terms 'perfect relation', one that supersedes and embraces all other relation—relation, in other words, with what we know as God. The Hasidic way is recognizably the way of religion. Buber's sets out to be that of religiousness, which may co-exist with religion but does not necessarily do so.

Another marked variant to come from this different ordering of a spiritual progress is that whereas Hasidism places at the side of the traveller a heavenly Lord in whom he feels secure, who accompanies him from the beginning to the end of his life, along the other way only intimations are given of his Presence, an awareness to which the voyager is eventually brought by dint of becoming attuned to the presence of the world and what goes on there. Much of this underlies the argument developed in *I and Thou* and will be discussed further in that connection. In this chapter, the intention is to explain what Buber saw in Hasidism and how he understood it.

At the root of Hasidic teaching on God is what is known as the doctrine of the sparks. 'One of the most amazing and far-reaching conceptions in the whole history of Kabbalism',[2] according to the foremost expert on Jewish mysticism, Gershom Scholem, this theory relating to the creation of the world offers an explanation of how the all-encompassing Nothingness of God could have given way to the Something that is the cosmos. Isaac Luria's contribution was founded on the ancient Kabbalist concept of *tsimtsum* or contraction of God. God, so the myth goes, contracted his Light, one of the synonyms of his Presence, like a person drawing in his breath, and in the darkness that ensued 'cut boulders and hewed rocks'.[3] God, that is to say, created space for what was not himself by shrinking into himself. He then called into existence Primordial Man, *Adam Kadmon*. This was not *homo sapiens* but a configuration of the Light flowing from *En-Sof, Without End*, a Kabbalistic name for God inspired by his infinity, which streamed from *Adam Kadmon*'s eyes, ears, mouth and nose. To catch this light, bowls had been placed at every quarter of the universe, but while some of them remained firm, the others shattered under the force of the Light pouring into them and sparks in their millions flew into every corner of creation, each becoming embedded in its own 'shell'. Moreover, when Adam was created, the first man of Genesis, his fall not only reactivated the drama of the sparks, but the light of his own soul dispersed in more sparks which flew similarly into exile together with the Light of *Without End*. The task now required is one of *tikkun*, or mending. The damage caused by the imprisonment of the sparks, those of man and those of the world, must be mended, the sparks helped to rejoin the Godhead to which they belong. As a Hasidic teacher said, the perfection and unification of God depends on man. His duty is not so much to save his own soul as to 'elevate heaven': the implication being that the accomplishment of the latter brings about the former, since the release of the fragmented hidden divine Presence demands a human unified presence with it. When God is reunited with his indwelling Presence, his *Shekhinah*, the whole of creation will be reunited into a unity of a life lived in the one Presence.

This correlation of divine destiny with that of man was a hallmark of the teaching of Rabbi Israel ben Eliezer, the Ba'al Shem Tov. His aim was to relate religious maxims and truths to the actualities of earthly life and what was known of the 'inmost heart'. In the Hasidic doctrine of God, allusions to the divine nature are expressly and repeatedly made to correspond to human characteristics in the belief, as Isaac Luria taught, that whatever is in God exists in embryo in human beings and is intended to grow and develop. Rabbi Mosheh of Kobryn could assert that he was able to recognize the unity of God in his unifying impact on himself. He explains the Passover riddle, 'One, who knows it? One, I know it', as follows.

> One, who knows it? Who can discern the Only One? The seraphim themselves ask: 'Where is the place of his Glory?' Nevertheless, one I know it. For as the sage [the medieval poet-philosopher Judah Halevi] says, 'Where do I find Thee and where do I not find Thee?' And the seraphim answer, 'The whole earth is full of His Glory' (Is. 6:3). I can discern the only One in what he does to me.[4]

Underlying this explication is once again the doctrine of the sparks, but its essentially Hasidic slant makes its appearance in the way the theological element is made to match the human condition. The unity and uniqueness of God are amenable to perception. As Buber says, Hasidism is Kabbalah become ethos.

How did the *zaddikim* think of God? A story is told of Rabbi Shneur Zalman, who died in 1813 after founding a Lithuanian branch of Hasidism called Habad, wherein more emphasis was laid on the intellect than in orthodox Hasidism. According to this, he once asked a student what God was. The student stayed mute. He asked him a second and a third time and still the student said nothing. Exasperated, he demanded why he did not answer. 'Because I don't know,' said the younger man. 'Do I know then?' asked the rabbi. 'Yet I have to say it, for this is what I have to say: he is plainly there, and apart from him nothing is plainly there, and *that* is what he is.'[5] For the rabbi, God's Presence was sure; it was precisely because of it that all else was endowed with presence. That nothing is there apart from him is tied to the Hasidic variant on the *tsimtsum* myth that when God 'shrank' into himself to leave room for the world, he did not merely call into being a world separate from himself. He caused it to exude out of himself like a snail from the shell made of its own substance. The passage from Deuteronomy (4:39), 'Know this day and lay it to your heart that YHWH* is God in

* These letters represent the Hebrew Tetragram, or the holiest divine Name which, according to Jewish tradition reaching back to late biblical times, it is forbidden to pronounce. It is read as 'Lord'.

heaven above and on the earth beneath. There is none else', really means that YHWH is the one and only God. But the *hasid* was instructed to read it as, 'There is nothing else.'

God created the world because he wished to be known, loved and desired. Longing for something beside himself, he radiated out of himself what are categorized as the spheres of separation, creation, formation and production; the worlds of ideas, forces, forms and matter; the realms of genius, spirit, soul and life. Accordingly, he wraps his destiny in layers and coverings, only the outermost of which has to do with man, but that is where the indwelling Presence, his *Shekhinah*, is banished. At that furthest point from the Godhead, it calls out to be returned to its 'root'. So in addition to the usual verticality of movement of the Godhead upward and downward, Hasidism sees a constant traffic from inside outward and vice versa, a process outward towards the *Shekhinah* and inward towards reunification of the created world and God within it. The Kabbalist suggests that the world of production is the one which meets the eyes. Explore it more deeply, unwrap the materiality, and you reach the world of formation. Unwrap still further and you come to the world of creation. Explore further still and you find the world of separation; 'until you come to *Without End*, blessed be he'.

Another feature of the Jewish mystical explanation of the creation of the world is the stress laid on speech. God 'spoke' the creation. It is a 'word' out of his mouth, one, furthermore, that he utters without ceasing. For with the dispersion of his Presence through the breaking of the bowls, countless millions of new 'mouths' have come into existence able to 'speak' new 'words'. God for Hasidism is the Speaker, the Lord of the Voice, who continuously expresses through the most unexpected channels his love, commands, interdictions, consolation and guidance. As Rabbi Meir of Ger said:

Scripture's account of the voice of Sinai that it 'added no more' (Deut. 5:22) is understood by the Targum[6] to mean that it continued without interruption. And indeed, the Voice speaks today as it did long ago. But to hear it, it is necessary, as it was then, to be prepared. As it is written, 'And now, if you will listen, listen to my voice' (Ex. 19:5), The now is this: when we listen to it.[7]

Belief in the ubiquity of God (of a kind not to be confused with pantheism), together with the characteristic Hasidic habit of bringing all religious speculation back to man himself, shows itself in a saying of a pupil of the Ba'al Shem, Rabbi Pinhas of Koretz. Asked why God is given the name of 'Place' in rabbinic literature, and not 'Place of the World', his answer was that it was because man 'should enter into God so that God encompasses him and becomes his place'.[8]

Yet, so the Ba'al Shem taught, consciousness of the omnipresence of God was not merely to be enjoyed passively. It was to serve as a call to action. His followers were to hear the Voice of the Presence crying for release from every house-wall and every cornfield, from every cart-horse and every cooking-pot, from every joy and every sorrow, from every job done and from everything that happened to them. Hasidism was to be a sanctification of the whole of life, in which the presence of its adherents with whatever was the vis-à-vis of the moment would enable them to distinguish and satisfy the needs of people, beasts and things, and conduce to their fulfilment by assisting them to become more fully what they are intended to be.

Every *hasid* was thus meant to be a helper. But the helper *par excellence* (after God the supreme Helper) was the *zaddik*.

A *zaddik*, before the term acquired its Hasidic sense, was simply a just man, a good man, a Jew at his best. *Hasid*, on the other hand, connotes pious, devout, and originally described the enthusiast, the inspired non-conformist innovator, even the extremist, one whose religious life was far more intense than that of a *zaddik*. Some of the ancient rabbis belonged to this category. So did Jesus.[9] However, with the foundation of the Hasidic movement, these two rather confusingly changed places. A *hasid* who took over the religious leadership of a community became known as a *zaddik*, and the *zaddikim* who attached themselves to him were given the title *hasidim*.

A *zaddik* was the pivot on which his congregation turned, the holy man close to God, competent to deal with problems big and small. He was the healer of soul and body, who knew of the effects of the one upon the other. He was a teacher to whom young men flocked from far and wide, who taught as much by example as by word of mouth. One *zaddik* said of his own teacher: 'I learnt Torah from all my teacher's limbs'.[10] Another described the ideal at which he aimed thus:

> A man should pay heed that all his actions are Torah, and that he himself becomes a Torah, until one learns from his habits and movements and motionless cleaving, and he becomes like the heavens of which it is said, 'No utterance at all, no speech, their voice is inaudible, yet their sound goes out over all the earth, their message to the end of the world' (Ps. 19:4).[11]

Each *zaddik* of the classical period of Hasidism was distinguished by some special talent. Some, like the Ba'al Shem himself, were men of immense magnetism. Some were strict ascetics, like Abraham the Angel who abjured sex. His wife dreamt after his death that she saw him entering a hall where the great were sitting on their thrones, and heard him confess that his wife had a grievance against him for this. 'I forgive you with all my heart,' she cried out in her sleep. A specially Hasidic touch is then given to the rest of the story, for instead of Rabbi Abraham being pardoned and offered a throne of his own, it relates that it was his wife who awoke comforted.

Other *zaddikim* were intense lovers of God. Aaron of Karlin was thought to be such a living fount of love that all who heard him pray were infected by it. It was nevertheless love tempered by fear, for he believed that without fear men love only an agreeable idol and not the great and terrible Lord. Elimelekh of Lizhensk (d. 1786) was also a passionate lover of God. He had to keep an eye on his watch while praying lest he should 'fly away for blessedness'. Similarly, for Rabbi Uri of Strelisk (d. 1822) prayer was so overwhelming that before setting out to pray in the morning he would put his house in order and say farewell to his wife and children.

Rabbi Nachman ben Simchai, the rabbi of Bratslav and a personality of the greatest weight in the Hasidic movement, about whom more will be said in chapter 3, was a person in profound sympathy with nature. He taught that every living creature has a language of its own and said that a horse need never be whipped if one has learned how to speak to it. He was incidentally not unique in this respect. Buber quotes many anecdotes to the effect that birds, beasts and even frogs were considered able to 'talk'. Nachman regretted that people are deaf to the songs which even the vegetable world sings to God, 'How lovely and sweet', he exclaimed on one occasion, 'it is to hear them singing! And therefore it is good to worship God among them, in lonely wandering in the countryside among the plants of the earth, and to pour out one's words to God in sincerity. All the words of the countryside then enter into your own and increase their strength.'[12] Fascinated by speech of every kind, Rabbi Nachman regarded the word as a precious mystery, and the act of teaching in particular, when the word travels to and fro between teacher and pupil, as a sort of miracle.

Other *zaddikim* were fine preachers like Shmelke of Nikolsburg (d. 1778). Others still were notable for their humility, like Meshullam Zusya of Hanipol (d. 1800). Meshullam once argued with his brother about how to gain some idea of the greatness of God. He thought the first step must be to realize one's own lowliness. Not so, replied the brother. Humility comes from contemplating Majesty. Their teacher decided that both were right but that—and again the distinctive Hasidic touch—'the inner grace is with one who begins with himself and not with the Creator'.[13]

Jacob Isaac of Lublin, also one of the movement's eminent *zaddikim*, possessed great powers of intuition. He could apparently not only read on people's foreheads the petitions they were bringing to him, but could see into their lives past, present and future.

In some cases, the reputation of a *zaddik* was associated with his teaching, one emphasizing the value of silence, another that of unity, and so on. The Jew, asserted Abraham of Stretyn (d. 1865), should be so much one man that each of his five senses can take over the functions of the other four.

In 'My Way to Hasidism',[14] Buber tells a little story of how he came to understand what it meant to be a *zaddik*. In 1910 or 1911, he was in a coffee-house in Czernovitz, not far from Sadgora. He had given a lecture and had afterwards gone with a group from his audience for refreshment and conversation. As they were talking together, a man approached him and after introducing himself sat down to hear what was being said. The time passed, and Buber asked him whether he could help him in any way; but the answer was in the negative and the man remained quietly there. In the end, since it had grown late, Buber enquired again if there was anything he wished to say to him. 'I would like to ask you a question,' the other replied shyly. He then proceeded to explain that his daughter had a young man, a law student, whom she wanted to marry: but was he a steady person? Buber was nonplussed, never having laid eyes on the individual in question. He hedged a little and said that he thought from what had been said of the prospective son-in-law that he was probably reliable. But had he a good head on his shoulders, his questioner wanted to know? And should he become a judge or a lawyer? Buber then answered straightforwardly that he had no idea, and even if he had, he would hardly be in a position to advise on such matters. The older man looked at him half sadly, half with understanding, and murmured with a deprecatory smile: 'Herr Doctor, you do not want to say'. He then thanked him and left. Buber comments on this experience that, droll though it was, it afforded him an insight into the role of the *zaddik*.

> I who am no *zaddik*, not secure in God but in peril before God, a man struggling ever anew for God's light and ever anew vanishing into God's abysses, nevertheless, when asked the trivial and responding with the trivial, experienced from within, for the first time, the true *zaddik*, who is asked after revelation and responds with revelation. I experienced him in his soul's fundamental relation to the world: in his responsibility.[15]

The *rebbe* may no longer possess the spiritual powers that he possessed in years past, but is it not possible, Buber wondered, that the office of *rebbe* holds the germ of 'future orders'? Is he not perhaps what he was once thought and appointed to be?

He speaks: and he knows that what he says is destiny. He does not have to decide over the destiny of countries and nations, but ever again over the course, small and great, of an individual life, so finite and yet so limitless. People come to him, and each requires him to say something, requires his help. And though the needs they bring him may be material and semi-material, in his world-view there is nothing material that cannot be elevated to spirit. And what he does for all of them is this: *he elevates their need before he appeases it*. He is thus helper in the spirit, teacher of the world's meaning, guide to the divine sparks. It is he, the perfect man, who matters to the world. It is he for whom the world waits, for whom it waits ever anew.[16]

3

EARLY WRITINGS

The five years spent by Buber (partly in Florence) in relative seclusion, occupied with his Hasidic material, saw the publication of *The Tales of Rabbi Nachman* in 1906, *The Legend of the Ba'al-Shem* in 1908, and in 1909 *Ecstatic Confessions*, an anthology of writings mostly by western Christian spiritual personalities, but also by Jewish, Sufi, Chinese and Hindu mystics. It was in general a period of heady enchantment with all things esoteric and other-worldly for Buber, for enthusiasms which he later came to moderate. For example, whereas in his foreword to the book on Rabbi Nachman he does not hesitate to label Hasidism 'the last and highest development of Jewish mysticism', he afterwards toned down the movement's mystical aspect and thought that he had earlier tended to render the Hasidic legends a little too freely.

A great-grandson of the Ba'al Shem Tov, Rabbi Nachman of Bratslav, the town where he ministered, chiefly focused his mystical longings and imaginings on the land of Israel. For him it was the place of the creation, and will be that of the world to come. Joy is there and perfect wisdom, and the perfect music of the world is there. The unity of the world is to derive from there and also the resurrection of the dead. So the perfect grave is there. Nachman used to say that his real life began with his journey to Israel in 1798, that all that he knew before that time was nothing at all, and that his earlier teachings should not be preserved.

He married at fourteen according to custom and left the town of his birth to live in the village where his father-in-law resided. The effect on him was overwhelming. Freed for the first time from the Jew's age-long alienation from nature, he no longer felt driven by an urge towards asceticism or by an inner struggle for greater closeness to God, for now he found God everywhere. All living things became dear to him. Once he slept in a house built of young trees and dreamt that he was lying among the dead. In the morning he complained to the house's owner. 'For,' as he told him, 'if one fells a tree before its time, it is as though one murders a living soul.'[1]

When Rabbi Nachman had been in Bratslav for five years he became ill with tuberculosis. But he was not afraid to die. He thought of death rather as moving to a higher stage in the great transmigration of souls to an ever newer and better form of life. He said, 'Whoever reaches true knowledge, knowledge of God, for him there is no division between life and death, for he adheres to God and embraces him and lives eternal life as he does.'[2]

In the work on the Ba'al Shem, the founder of Hasidism is depicted in accordance with Buber's mood of the time as the author of miracles and strange happenings, a somewhat different figure, in effect, from the person met in Buber's writings of later years. His real contribution to Jewish spirituality is represented as being that he broke with the traditional Kabbalist pattern of separating the religious from 'the world' and rejected the pretension that the Kabbalistic religious exercises were meritorious in themselves. By the same token, as has been said, the Ba'al Shem breathed new life into those Kabbalistic teachings which brought support and encouragement to his hard-pressed fellow-Jews and invested their lives with a dignity and meaning which even the less intelligent among them could understand and appreciate.

Besides its collection of tales, *The Legend of the Ba'al-Shem* contains a section devoted to 'The Life of the Hasidim' which is of special value to Buber's understanding of Hasidism in that it sets out the six major Hasidic counsels of perfection: namely, *cleaving* (the literal meaning of the Hebrew *devekut*), *humility, holy intention, worship, ardour* and *joy.*

To *cleave* to God is to demonstrate love of God as it is described in the book of Joshua, when he orders the tribes of Reuben and Gad, and the half-tribe of Manasseh, to obey the law of Moses, which is 'to love the LORD your God and to walk in all his ways and to cleave to him and to serve him with all your heart and with all your soul' (Josh. 22:5). The early Kabbalists understood *cleaving* to demand a corresponding detachment from everything other than God. Thus Nachmanides in the thirteenth century could exhort his hearers not to divert their thought from God in all their doings.

> Such a man may be talking to other people, but his heart is not with them since he is in the presence of God. And it is further plausible that those who have attained to this rung do, even in their earthly life, partake of eternal life, because they have made themselves a dwelling-place of the *Shekhinah*.[3]

Perfect *cleaving* thus entailed, as the culmination of the way of holiness, a positive turning away from attachment to the world. To this the Ba'al Shem introduced a radical change. *Cleaving* for him signified the first rung of the ladder to holiness. Moreover, it was not an intellectual or spiritual exercise reserved for the élite, but within the competence of every Jew. *Cleaving* for the Hasidim was to be conscious of the Presence of God in all the things, events and encounters of everyday life. As Gershom Scholem writes, in his own explanation of *cleaving*, 'to be aware of this real omnipresence and immanence of God is already the realization of the state of *devekut*.'[4] Yet if *cleaving* was the beginning of the spiritual life of the Hasid, it nevertheless also remained its end. Buber reports the Ba'al Shem as having said:

> Consider the person who day in and day out rushes about on his business in the market through the streets. He almost forgets that there is a Creator of the world. Not until it is time to pray *Minchah* [the afternoon prayer] does it occur to him, 'I must pray.' But then he sighs from the bottom of his heart because his day has been spent in such futility, and he runs into a side street and stands and prays. He is held dear, very dear, before God, and his prayer pierces the heavens.[5]

Cleaving was a state of being-with-God, but it alternated with apparent interludes of apartness from God. Rabbi Yechiel

Mikhal taught that this must be expected.

> We read in the psalm, 'Who may ascend the mountain of
> YHWH and who may stand in the place of his holiness?'
> (Ps. 24:3) This is to be compared to a man who travels up
> a mountain in his cart, and when half way up, his horses
> are tired and he has to stop so that they can get their
> breath. Now a person without discernment will roll down
> at that point. But the discerning takes a stone and wedges
> it under the cart while it is stationary. He can thus reach
> the top of the mountain. Whoever does not fall when he
> has to interrupt his worship, but knows how to remain
> standing, he will ascend the mountain of the Lord.[6]

Humility has a slightly different connotation from that
generally intended. Alive to the need to love and respect the
self, Hasidism invests *humility* with none of the self-denigration
and humiliation with which it tends to be associated elsewhere.
On the contrary, the *hasid* is told that the gravest sin he can
commit is to forget that he is the child of the king. But he is not
to be proud: pride is one of the divine attributes which he is not
to imitate. He is to remember always that he is merely one
among many. Each is a part and none the whole. In Buber's
words:

> The individual sees God and embraces Him. The indi-
> vidual redeems the fallen worlds. And yet the individual is
> not a whole, but a part. And the purer and more perfect
> he is, so much the more intimately does he know that he is
> a part, and so much the more actively there stirs in him
> the community of existence. That is the mystery of
> humility.[7]

Another characteristic adduced to Hasidic *humility* by Buber
is that it is not pursued as an end in itself but as a means of
fulfilling the greater obligation of love. It is encouraged not as
an abasement of the human self in order to throw into relief the
greatness of God, but as a lowering of the self into the 'depths'
in order to confirm by its presence there God's own Presence.
To quote Rabbi Uri of Strelisk:

We read in the psalm, 'If I climb to heaven, You are there, if I make my bed in the realm of the tombs, there You are' (Ps. 139:8). If I imagine myself to be great and to move in heaven, I find that God is a faraway 'there', and the higher I reach, the further away he is. But if I make my bed in the depths and humble myself to the lowest world, there He is, with me.[8]

A further anecdote illustrating *humility* appears in Buber's *Tales of the Hasidim*. A sad countryman asked Rabbi Mosheh Leib if he loved him. But of course, answered the rabbi. The other was however still quite unsure, for if the rabbi was really fond of him he would know what ailed him without being told.

'Thus,' runs the tale, 'lives the humble man, who is righteous and loving and a helper: mingling with all, yet untouched by all, devoted to the many yet collected within his own singleness, fulfilling on the rocky summit of solitude a covenant with the Infinite, and in the valley of life a covenant with those on earth.'[9]

Holy intention as a counsel of perfection concerns the correlation of the inner man with the outer practice of his religion. The '*holy intention* of the heart', as it is sometimes known, is a turning of the mind, which in ancient Judaism is seated in the heart, to God. 'Man looks on the outward appearance but YHWH looks on the heart' (1 Sam. 16:7). 'The Holy One, blessed be He, demands the heart,' says the Talmud.[10] This wider scope of *holy intention* shrank under the influence of the Kabbalists to the smaller one of prayer and ritual observances in which the believer was expected to concentrate wholly and entirely on what was said or written. Again, the early *hasidim* transformed this intellectual element of *holy intention* so that it came very closely to resemble *cleaving*.

Interestingly, a distinction was made between the 'intention of receiving' and the 'intention of giving'. With the help of the first, life is accepted as coming from God, and all things with which the *hasid* comes into contact are seen as needing to be treated with the greatest care and respect because of the sparks in them of God's Presence. It should be added, too, that the 'intention of receiving' was thought to affect not only the things of this world but also souls, and in particular the souls of those who die without having reached perfection and become whole. According to Kabbalistic teaching, which Hasidism inherited, these wander from world to world seeking opportunities to mend whatever was damaged in former lives so that their soul-sparks, which all have their root in Adam and were scattered at the Fall, may be reunified with the First Soul.

With regard to the 'intention of giving', Buber's explication of it, and its connection with meditation, is not too easy to follow because he does not deal fully enough with the Hasidic sources he cites. But in 'intention of giving', absorption in the written or spoken word should be such as though the 'heavens were opened in them. And as though it were not that you take the word into your mouth, but as though you enter into the word.'[11] One, that is to say, who 'enters into' a passage which he has heard or read in such a way that he perceives its meaning, and who recommunicates it in a new literary or spoken form, is equipped to recreate for the external world the discovery that he has made within himself. To become a creator of this sort he must, however, himself first become a new creation. To become Something, he must arrive at Nothing. 'And then God creates a new creation in him and he is as a source which does not run dry and as a stream which does not fail.'[12]

As Buber accounts for it, *holy intention* has two faces and one role in Hasidism. As an 'intention of receiving' it participates in the redemption of the world by being concerned with the use, handling and consumption of things in holiness. It contributes to the realization of the inner value and dignity of what is external. As an 'intention of giving', it participates in the same redemption by being concerned with making and creating things in holiness, by giving external expression to what is internal. For in the last resort, according to Buber, it is through holy making and holy use that the redemption of the world is to be effected.

Worship was for many ages associated with institutional and communal *worship* in the Temple, but after it was destroyed the rabbis taught that this was to be replaced by '*worship* of the heart'. And what is *worship* of the heart? 'This is prayer.'[13] At the beginning of time, prayer was simply a matter of God calling and man answering. It was enough for Adam to hear the sound of God walking in the Garden, and for Moses to hear the Voice, for a dialogue between man and God to come into being. Hasidism recognized all the various stages of relation between man and God expressed in *worship* but added to the biblical record its own special quality of religious existentialism and inwardness. Where the Bible writes, 'And Abel brought, he too . . .' (Gen. 4:4), Rabbi Uri of Strelisk interpreted this to mean that Abel brought his 'he' to God. It is this, Uri taught, that makes a person's offering acceptable to God. Similarly, Mosheh of Kobryn, praying, 'Lead us into our land, there we will bring to You the offerings of our obligations', interrupted himself and cried out: 'Lord of the world, we, we, we ourselves! We desire to bring ourselves to You.'[14] Another rabbi said that when a *hasid* prayed, he was to bind himself in his mind to all Israel. At the same time, in all true prayer a person prays alone. The great subject of prayer, it will be unnecessary to remark at this juncture, was for the reunion of God and his *Shekhinah*, his indwelling Presence. A *hasid* was taught that his sorrows and troubles sprang from the sadness and exile of the divine Presence.

> Through his own need and deficiency he learns the deficiency of the *Shekhinah*, to pray that the deficiencies of the *Shekhinah* may be made good, and that through him, the praying man, the union may occur of God and His *Shekhinah* . . . For everything above and below is one unity.[15]

Ardour, which in Hebrew, as in English, derives from the root 'to burn', clearly refers to the phenomenon recognized as ecstasy, of which, together with trances and other such mystical extremes, Buber eventually came to disapprove. There is however no denying that for the *hasidim* these were experiences through which the devotee passed as he progressed step by step along the path to holiness. The Ba'al Shem himself was

noted for his moments of ecstasy, when he would be seized by a
fit of trembling as he prayed, and his face 'shone like a torch,
and the eyes were wide open and staring like those of a dying
man'.[16] Rabbi Shmelke of Nikolsburg, in his turn, broke into
liturgical chants with 'new melodies, miracle of miracles, which
he had never heard before, nor had any other human ear. And
he had no idea of what he was singing, or how, since he was
bound to the world above.'[17]

Besides the burning of ecstasy, *ardour* meant for the *hasid* a
'burning enthusiasm' for God whose Presence is everywhere. As
Rabbi Nachman taught:

> Purity of heart is attained through having the heart on fire
> for God, blessed be He. Through this is the heart purified.
> For if a man is to counter his burning and glowing in sin
> or evil lusts, God forbid, through which his heart becomes
> unclean, he must set his heart on fire to burn for God,
> blessed be He. As it is written, 'All that has been through
> fire you shall pass through fire' (Num. 31:23).[18]

Because God is known as 'the Place' of the world, *ardour*
embraces him in the world. A *zaddik* said that there are two
kinds of love, the love of a man for his wife, which is
consummated in secret, and love for relations and children,
which needs no concealment. In the same way, there are two
kinds of love of God. There is love by way of the Torah, prayer
and fulfilling the commandments, which is consummated
quietly so as not to lead to vainglory and pride. And there is
love in time, when a person mixes with others, gives and takes,
listens and speaks, and secretly *cleaves* to God. 'And the latter is a
higher stage than the former. And it is said of it, "Who gives
You to me as a brother who suckled at my mother's breasts!
Were I to find You in the street, I would kiss You, and they
would not be able to mock me."'[19]

The sixth counsel of perfection is *joy*; but this is not
particular to Hasidism. Music, song, dancing, exultation, recur
constantly in the Bible, where God himself is projected as a God
of joy rejoicing in his creation. Indeed, *joy* is considered so

essential, and the recommendations to partake with enjoyment of what God has provided so traditional, that *joy* is sometimes represented as the key to the Hebrew cult. Certainly, there was a bias against asceticism even in its moderate forms, Rabbi Akiva, the renowned second-century teacher and martyr, holding that it was not permissible to inflict harm of any kind on oneself. The *zaddikim*, despite the depth added to the significance of *joy* by Kabbalah, followed rather the purity of the biblical meaning. The *hasid* rejoiced in all that he did as prescribed by Deuteronomy 'You shall rejoice in the LORD your God in all that you undertake' (Deut. 12:18). He ate and drank with *joy*; prayed, worked and made love with *joy*. He worshipped with *joy*, dancing and singing, he even smoked his pipe with *joy*. And he died with *joy*. When the daughter of Menachem Mendel of Rymanov succumbed to illness shortly after the death of his wife, he turned to God and prayed:

'Lord of the world, You have taken my wife from me. Yet I could still have rejoiced in my daughter. Now You have taken her too and I can rejoice in You alone. Therefore, I will rejoice in You.' And he recited the main prayer of the Sabbath in a transport of joy.[20]

Yet although the *hasid* rejoiced in the world, it was not because of the world but because of God. He played his fiddle and danced because of the divine Presence he believed to be there. The aim was to make God joyful, to make God 'sing'. As Rabbi Elimelekh interpreted the words of the psalm, 'For it is good to sing to our God' (Ps. 147:1), the meaning is, 'It is good when a man manages to make God sing within him.'[21]

Such are the major counsels of perfection in Hasidism as they appear (in English) in *The Legend of the Ba'al-Shem*, *Hasidism and Modern Man* and in Buber's two volumes of *The Tales of the Hasidim*. Five secondary counsels, originally published in Hebrew in 1945, are given in *Hasidism and Modern Man* and *The Way of Man according to the Teachings of Hasidism*, under the titles of 'heart-searching', 'resolution', 'beginning with oneself', 'not to be preoccupied with oneself', 'here where one stands', and 'the particular way'. They do not, strictly speaking, belong to the earlier period of Buber's career, but are given here to round off his treatment of Hasidism.

Briefly, *heart-searching* is once more closely associated with consciousness of the *Shekhinah*. Rabbi Baruch of Mezbizh, meditating on Ps. 132:4, 'I will not give sleep to my eyes nor slumber to my eyelids until I find a place for YHWH', comments, 'until I find myself and establish myself as a place prepared for the descent of the *Shekhinah*'.[22]

Resolution, the reverse, of course, of irresolution or vacillation, has mainly to do with the obligation of the *hasid* to carry through whatever has been started until it is finished.

Beginning with oneself. While the *hasid* was advised to know himself, he was also taught to put his own house in order before trying to set the world to rights. Rabbi Bunam counselled: 'Not until a man has found peace in himself can he go out to seek it in the world.'[23]

In being advised *not to be preoccupied with himself*, the *hasid* was warned against the dangers of self-absorption, one of them being that it can lead to ill-health. The rabbi of Ger exhorted his congregation on the Day of Atonement, when the Jews confess their sins and ask for pardon, not to dwell inordinately on wrongs done, for 'one's soul is well and truly there in whatever one thinks'. A person is present in his own baseness. Besides, he becomes depressed. The sensible advice therefore is: 'Stir the mud here, stir the mud there. Sinned or not sinned, what does heaven get out of it? While I ruminate over it, I can string pearls for heaven's joy. Turn from evil completely, do not brood on it, and do what is good.'[24]

As for *here where one stands*, the counsel is that each should aim at holiness in his own place, which is itself sanctified by the sparks of the indwelling Presence which look to him for their release. Nothing leads to more satisfactory fulfilment than to live in real and true relationship with the people, creatures and things of one's own environment. When a *zaddik* asked some learned men where God dwells, they laughed and said the whole world is full of his Glory. He would not accept this slick reply. According to him, God takes up his residence where he is admitted, and the only dwelling-place that the individual is qualified to offer him is the place and the situation in which he actually finds himself.

The particular way. Here the teaching, according to Buber, is that every man must follow his own path to God, must develop his own powers. The Rabbi Jacob Isaac of Lublin, known as 'the Seer', when asked for one general way to serve God, replied that it is not a matter of saying to someone which way he should take, for there is a way to serve God through teaching, through praying, through fasting and through eating. 'Each should take careful note of the way to which his heart draws him and then choose it with all his might.'[25] This simple and pleasant recipe is typically Hasidic: by serving God in his own way a person helps to perfect his own self. Choosing to offer to God what he does best, he fulfils the duty of every Jew to utilize his abilities to their full capacity. Rabbi Yechiel Mikhal of Zloczov observed:

> It is the duty of every man in Israel to know and consider that in his nature he is unique in the world and that there has never been another like him. For had there been another like him, he would not need to be in the world. Each individual is a new thing in the world and must perfect his own nature in this world. For truly, it is because this does not happen that the coming of the Messiah is delayed.[26]

Buber returned to public life in 1909 on the invitation of a Zionist student group in Prague, the Bar Kochba Verein, to give the first of a series of three yearly talks. Thus began an association which lasted for several years and was of much importance both to him and to the society's members, some of whom remained attached to him for the rest of their lives. Led by Hugo Bergman, who later became the first rector of the Hebrew University of Jerusalem, the Bar Kochba group consisted mainly of young people from an assimilated, financially and professionally settled, thoroughly westernized background, estranged from Judaism. For them, Buber's message was novel, exciting and inspiring and he became their leader and mentor. He also deeply influenced through his contact with Bar Kochba the philosophy and Jewish outlook of such writers and thinkers as Max Brod,[27] Franz Kafka and many others.

But if Hugo Bergman prepared the way, as he did, for the Prague encounter with Buber, another two members of the society who made their name in the world of letters, Hans Kohn and Robert Weltsch, consolidated it with their writings and their friendship. Indeed, it is some indication of how greatly Buber impressed the Zionist youth of Prague of those years before the First World War that Robert Weltsch's *Nachwort*, his 1961 postscript to the study written by Hans Kohn in 1930 covering the first fifty years of Buber's life, closes with an extract from the latter's third address to the Bar Kochba society delivered fifty years earlier. Apropos of Buber's words at the end of *Gog und Magog*[28] to the effect that we have as yet in this 'desolate night' in which we live no way to point to, but must stand firm, with a ready soul, for when the morning dawns and a way at last becomes visible where none suspected it to lie, Weltsch adds a passage from Buber which he still remembered from so long ago:

> We know that it will come, we do not know how it will come. We can only be ready ... To be ready means to make ready.[29]

The lectures, which he pubished in 1911 as *Drei Reden über das Judentum* (*Three Addresses on Judaism*), are homiletic in style and worthy of a thoughtful and intelligent rabbi, which of course Buber was not. Curiously, they contain few signs of the mystical material on which he had been working for so long, but it is easy to recognize the still fully living impression made on him by Hasidism in the way he drives home the themes of renewal, deed and unity.

The first lecture 'Judaism and the Jews', discusses integrity. Living in an environment alien to his nature and religious tradition, the Jew is subjected to a duality which tears him apart. Is there such a thing nowadays as genuine Jewish religiousness, or do we call ourselves Jews merely because our ancestors did so? The Jew must choose between the various claims made on him. He must become a whole and unified person in the world in which he lives.

Continuing with the notion of integrity, the second address, 'Judaism and Mankind', argues that beside integrity towards his surroundings, the Jew must achieve integrity within his own self. Jewish literature and history abounds with characters in whom virtue jostles for a place beside vice, where purest self-sacrifice cohabits with arrant selfishness, noblest sincerity with darkest duplicity. Yet no nation had struggled more valiantly for unity than the Jews, for the unity of the person, of the person and the nation, of mankind, unity of God and of the world. Redemption from duality, Buber insists in these pages, is a Jewish idea. In the times of the prophets and of early Christianity, the Jew presented the world with a religious synthesis; in the age of Spinoza, with a synthesis of ideas; in the age of Socialism, with a social synthesis. What synthesis was the spirit of Judaism preparing in 1910?

The third in this initial group of lectures to the Prague students pleads for a return to the realities of Jewish religious life, for a *teshuvah* or turning back to true religiousness. Just as heaven and earth are to be 'created anew', in the words of Isaiah, so must the Jew be renewed. He possesses a feeling for unity which enables him to envisage an association of things rather than each individually; he tends to see the wood better than the trees. He inclines towards action rather than perception; his doing is more efficient than his perceiving, and in religion his deed is central rather than his experience. He is disposed towards the future because he has a stronger concept of time than of space. Translate these talents and ideals into reality, Buber tells the young people, and a new universalism will come into being. But first the Jew must become unified in himself; and to prepare the way for action he must first realize his own potential for action.

The remaining work of substance to be published before the First World War was *Daniel*, which appeared in 1913.[30] A mercifully short composition quite different again from the Prague addresses and the Hasidic writings—much more German and romantic in tone—it takes the form of five conversations between a certain Daniel and five different partners and marks Buber's gradual transition to the more mature outlook expressed eventually in *I and Thou*. In one dialogue, for example, Daniel tells his companion that she must fight free of the many and discover the one, the one direction that she must follow, the one intended for her, the one that is not 'over things nor around things nor between things, but in each thing, in the experience of each thing'.[31] If, that is, she stands back from a tree, she will derive a great deal of information concerning it, but she will not get to know it until its cones become her children, its bark her skin, and so on. The same parable re-emerges in *I and Thou* but without the recommended identification of the *I* with the tree, or the advice to 'experience' it. Similarly, the two opposing concepts defined in *Daniel* as 'realization' and 'orientation' are replaced later by the stands of *I-you* and *I-it*. To 'realize', to invest with reality, signified for Buber the association of an object, person or event with nothing other than itself, whereas 'orientation' meant the attitude he later named *I-it*, the attribution of qualities, values and dimensions to things, persons and events. 'Realization' remained very much part of Buber's vocabulary, but not 'orientation'.

Another of Daniel's friends complains that his life seems meaningless and he is afraid. Daniel's advice to him is that if he sets out in the direction he believes to be right, and tries to experience every event and every encounter as authentically as he can, he will discover that each has a message for him. The star of meaning will then shine over his existence. For meaning is not solid and stable. It is forged out of the elements, like Elijah's chariot.

> 'Danger, danger, danger!' Daniel tells him. 'Let your motto be God and danger! For danger is the gateway to profound reality, and reality is the supreme reward of life and the everlasting birth of God ... You have no security in the world, but you have direction and meaning. And God who desires to be realized, the God of the daring, is near you always.'[32]

It must not, in the light of what later happened to the Jews in Germany, come as too much of a shock that during the war years Buber wore the hat of a German patriot. It would be only too easy to assemble testaments of love for the land and its people published in those days by some of Jewry's best-known figures (Georg Simmel and Hermann Cohen among them). There is the story, typical but true, of a newly-married orthodox couple from Odessa who travelled to southern Germany for their honeymoon and put up in a strictly kosher hotel. On the day that war was declared, the hotel-keeper, himself a Jew of course, marched into the dining-room wearing a spiked helmet and brandishing a sword, and ordered all the 'enemy aliens' out of the house forthwith. Martin Buber was therefore in this respect simply a man of his period and place. Admittedly, not all were similarly infected. Gustav Landauer, Buber's great friend, reacted with horror to some of his remarks. In one address, for instance, on 'The Spirit of the Orient and Judaism', Buber committed the following to paper:

> I would define the Oriental type of human being, recognizable in the documents of Asia's antiquity as well as in the Chinese or Indian or Jew of today, as a man of pronounced motor faculties, in contrast to the Occidental type, represented by, say, the Greek of the Periclean period, the Italian of the Trecento, or the contemporary German, whose sensory faculties are greater than his motor.[33]

Unable to contain himself, Landauer wrote to Buber, 'I confess my blood boils when I read how you place "the contemporary German" side by side with the Greeks of the age of Pericles and the Italians of the Trecento.' To do him justice, Buber deleted from the second edition of the address in 1919 his original call to the German nation to lead the way to a new *teshuvah*. But Landauer's fury that he should have looked on Germany as the new Redeemer-Nation had been enormous. It was, however, *teshuvah* that was the principal focus of Buber's thought in those times, and not the fortunes and misfortunes of the *Heimat*. Indeed, he was attacked by Landauer on this score also, for viewing 'community' as one of the finer outcomes of the war.

Besides founding (in 1916) and editing a monthly, *Der Jude*, Buber, who was financially independent thanks to an income from his father's estate, produced a few minor pieces just before the end of the war, and immediately following it, such as 'My Way to Hasidism' and 'The Holy Way', the latter dedicated to the recently murdered Landauer. But the most fateful event as far as his career was concerned was the establishment of a firm friendship with Franz Rosenzweig, whom he had first met in 1914. Rosenzweig, a German-Jewish theologian mainly known for his work *The Star of Redemption*, had served at the front during the war and afterwards taken over the direction of a Jewish college in Frankfurt-am-Main known as the Freies Jüdisches Lehrhaus, remaining its head until the progressive paralysis which robbed him gradually of mobility and speech and eventually killed him, made itself manifest. One day, because of his pleasure at a show of independence of spirit on Buber's part in connection with an affair in which he and Rosenzweig, with others, were implicated, Rosenzweig suddenly felt the urge to renew the early acquaintance, and in the course of a visit to Buber and his wife at their home in Heppenheim, not far from Frankfurt, he broached the idea of Buber's joining the staff at the Lehrhaus. He had realized, he said in a very long letter in December 1922 to the German art historian Rudolf Hallo, who succeeded him as principal of the Lehrhaus, that 'Buber was even intellectually not the mystical subjectivist people imagined him to be, but that even intellectually he had begun to develop into a solid and reasonable person.' 'I was quite thrilled,' Rosenzweig went on, 'by the great honesty with which he expressed himself.'[34]

Shortly afterwards, a letter came from Buber accepting the invitation to teach. It had been written to his own very great surprise, Buber assured him, since he had for years been turning down similar requests. In 1922 he spoke in the Lehrhaus on 'Religion as Presence' and held classes on Hasidic texts, as planned with Rosenzweig when they were together in Heppenheim. In 1923 he discussed 'The primal forms of religious life' (magic, sacrifice, mystery and prayer) and devoted his classes to 'Witnesses of religious lands from the east and from Judaism to

Christianity'. Next he spoke on prayer and, in the first term of
1925, on the Ba'al Shem Tov. Other themes followed, and in
1926, to the consternation of many, he collaborated with a
Christian pastor, Hermann Schafft, in a debate before his Jewish
students on 'Judaism and Christianity'.

In 1925, Buber was also made responsible for a course on
Jewish religion and ethics at Frankfurt University. Promoted to
a titular professorship of religion in 1930, he was obliged to
leave his post there in 1933.

Earlier, in 1921, Buber had attended the 12th Zionist
Congress at Karlsbad, the first to meet since the end of the First
World War, and had criticized Chaim Weizmann, the then
President of the Zionist Organization, for doing too little to
foster good relations with the Arabs. Robert Weltsch, also, had
asked point blank whether Zionists wanted a war with them or
not. The resolution Buber presented to the Congress ran as
follows:

The Jewish people have experienced with sorrow and
indignation the events of recent times. The hostile attitude
of sections of the Arab population of Palestine, prompted
by unscrupulous elements, which has ended in the outbreak of bloody deeds of violence, can neither weaken our
determination to construct a Jewish national home, nor
our will to live with the Arab people in a relationship of
concord and mutual respect, and with them to make a
common homeland into a flourishing community, the
building of which will ensure to each of its peoples
undisturbed national development. The two great Semitic
peoples, already once closely bound in common cultural
production, will understand in the hour of their national
re-birth, how to unite their life interests into a joint
undertaking.

The 12th Zionist Congress calls on the executive to
pursue their endeavours to reach a sincere understanding
with the Arab people on the basis of this statement, and
the safeguarding to an increased degree of the Balfour
Declaration. The Congress expressly emphasizes that

Jewish work of colonization will not encroach on the rights and needs of the Arab working people.[35]

Buber's idealistic propositions could not be rejected outright in case it might be thought that the Zionists intended to bear down on the Arabs, but his text was progressively emasculated, leaving him greatly disappointed and even dejected, as will be seen in chapter 6 from the letter which he wrote twenty-six years later to Judah Magnes.

Ernst Simon, who was to become a renowned education-alist and writer, was also present at the Congress and has testified to Buber's part in the debate. As Simon understood him, Buber was requiring that the Jews should contribute to the progress of the Arabs rather than turn them into enemies. To Simon, it was Buber who at that time appeared the *Realpolitiker*, and he never forgot Buber's words, to the extent that they became for him one of the factors which determined his own Zionism.

4

I AND THOU

'I have read your little book, confided to me before publication, with beating heart. You have done something good... The little book is too clear, and therefore in clarity not yet enough. It conveys still too light a shudder in face of the ineffable.'[1] Thus Florens Christian Rang, a Christian pastor, to Buber in September 1922. Or again, the French existentialist philosopher Gabriel Marcel, in a substantial assemblage of papers dedicated to Buber's writings: 'I am particularly delighted that their collective tribute to that great thinker, Martin Buber, affords me an opportunity to express my admiration for the priceless little book, *I and Thou*.'[2]

This 'little book', consisting of a mere one hundred and twenty pages (plus a postscript added in 1957 of another seventeen pages), is Buber's most famous work, the one to which he mainly owes his reputation. Within its small compass, he manages to trace a path through relation and absence of relation, to the unity and reality of the human *I*, and on to the binding up of a life of relation within what he calls perfect relation, relation with God.

The book was seven years in gestation, Buber told Franz Rosenzweig in a letter. It was given its first outline in May 1916, its first rough draft in the autumn of 1916, and its final form in the spring of 1922, when he was teaching at the Lehrhaus. In fact the 1922 version was not to be the definitive one: in a subsequent edition, as will be seen later, he introduced a small but far-reaching change into the text of part 3 of the book.

Its language, 'unique in the history of philosophy' in the words of Gershom Scholem, is in places a sort of prose poetry, though elsewhere quite straightforward, but clear though it may be, it calls for much concentration and more than one perusal. For some the style is a stumbling block, especially as it appears in the English language. The translation of Ronald Gregor Smith, who was the first on the scene in 1937, and whose rendering has come out since in one further edition and several reissues, omits the change alluded to, and preserves the original and superseded text of the passage in question. Its English is in any case stiff and graceless. The second translation, by Walter Kaufmann, is in some respects, or so it may be thought, an improvement in that in the text, although not in the title, 'you' is substituted for the archaic 'thou', and Buber's alteration makes its appearance at last (this being 1970). In other respects, Kaufmann succeeds at times in making Buber sound so ridiculous—one of the points which he makes in his long introduction, which in part apes Buber's language, is *mundus vult decipi*, the world wishes to be deceived, the implication being that Buber complies with the world's wish—that one returns almost with relief to the clumsy but at least respectful sobriety of R. Gregor Smith. (The references in this chapter and elsewhere are all to the older version.)

I would take this opportunity to mention that I, too, am using 'you' and 'You' in the following synopsis of the *I and Thou* text, while keeping 'Thou' in the title. The German word *du* implies an intimacy and familiarity admittedly not contained in 'you', but 'thou' in English is now addressed almost exclusively to the Deity. The impression is therefore given that the book is about man and God, which is quite misleading, though it is *also* about man and God. In the circumstances, it would no doubt be logical to alter the title to *I and You*, as I have done in a previous book,[3] but I am advised that on the whole it is less confusing to stay with the traditional title.

The point of departure of what has become known as the life of dialogue is that it presents us with alternative stands: relation and irrelation. I can, that is to say, either take up my place alongside whatever confronts me and in Buber's language address it as 'you': or I can hold myself apart from it and view it as an object, an 'it'. Furthermore, with each of these two attitudes I deploy a different *I*, the *I* of *I-you* being quite different from that of *I-it*. The first is an *I* caught up in exclusive relation, for a *you* can never be one 'something' among others; it must always be unique. The *I* of *I-it* by contrast, is one that experiences, assesses, compares, sums up, analyses and learns. Nothing of this kind comes between an *I* and its *you*; no anticipations, no preconceptions, no purposes, no aims, no desires. I cannot say *you* until these intermediate thoughts and feelings have disappeared. At the same time, nothing derogatory attaches to the stand of irrelation. On the contrary, without it I should not survive: it is from the *it*-world that I draw whatever knowledge, judgement and progress that I possess and enjoy—as long, that is to say, as the *I-you* of relation is the stronger of the two. It is essential that I have the ability to enter easily and frequently into relation, even to the extent that my life may be described as one of *I-you* rather than of *I-it*.

One feature of *I-you* relation is, however, its transience. It flows and ebbs and flows back again. Nothing exists that cannot become *you* for me, but inevitably it will withdraw sooner or later to the separation of an *it*. The only *you* which can never become for me an *it*, for the simple reason that I am unable to scrutinize it objectively, is the *You* I address to God; which is why, and not because of any attribute judged particular to the Deity, Buber describes it as the 'everlasting' *You*. 'God' can be drawn into the world of *it* and made the object of thought and speculation, but never the hidden divine *I*, the Mystery to whom my human *I* addresses itself.

Two further points. Firstly, relation always entails reciprocity. I affect my *you* and my *you* affects me, even when this is imperceptible to either or both.

Secondly, relation sometimes leads to encounter. From Buber's rather lax use of the two different nouns relation (*Beziehung*) and encounter (*Begegnung*), it is sometimes overlooked that these are not synonyms. He does in fact explicitly distinguish between them, but not emphatically enough, and certainly not consistently enough, and is therefore himself largely responsible for whatever uncertainty exists. But he made himself quite clear to Gabriel Marcel when the latter expressed worry about the suitability of the word *Beziehung* for the sense Buber intended. If relation is to be understood as a 'connection between two terms', or between 'data capable of being treated as terms', how, he asked Buber, can *I* and *you* be thought of in this way? Surely, *Begegnung*, encounter, was the better word. Buber replied:

> The question is asked whether the German term 'Beziehung' (rendered more or less accurately by 'relationship' in English), and in particular the French word 'relation', correspond to what I mean, where discontinuity is an essential element. The question is a valid one, and it is quite understandable that the term 'Begegnung' (encounter) should be thought more suitable. But 'Begegnung' signifies only something actual. A person who remains with someone he has encountered, encountered him in effect earlier. But the event is over; he no longer encounters him. The concept of 'Beziehung' by contrast, opens up the possibility—only a possibility but a possibility nonetheless—of latency. Two friends, two lovers, must repeatedly experience how *I-you* is succeeded by *I-him* or *I-her*, but does it not often seem in those moments as though a bird with a broken wing is trying secretly to fly? And does not an incomprehensible and, as it were, vibrating continuity manifest itself at times between *you*-moments? In the relationship of the true believer to God, the latent *You* is unmistakable; even when he is unable to turn to him with a wholly collected soul, the Presence of God is primordially real to him. One can only try to overcome the lack of an adequate designation by combining the skeleton-word 'Beziehung' with other more concrete and restricted terms such as 'Begegnung', contact, communication, depending on the context. It can be replaced by none of them.[4]

It would follow from Buber's answer that encounter is not, like relation, an attitude of mind, a psychological stage, but an event, something that happens. Nor, as some writers appear to have thought (e.g. Malcolm Diamond and Emmanuel Levinas), is relation a realization of encounter or grounded in encounter, the corollary being that encounter comes first (as would seem natural) and relation second. The very reverse is the case; relation comes first. This may seem strange, considering that encounter represents the high peak of relational life, the lightning flash which suddenly illumines the way. But it is 'only something actual'. In relation, by comparison, the moving backward to a position of *I-it* may possibly be the prelude to a new movement towards *I-you*.

As for what precisely is meant by encounter: whereas relation is the unilateral recognition of a vis-à-vis as *you* on the part of an *I*, encounter is what happens when two *I*'s step into relation simultaneously. Encounter is the coming together into existential communion of two *I*'s and two *you*'s. Encounter is a privilege that I receive. I enter into *you*-relation of my own accord and thereby fulfil the 'act of my being, my being's act';[5] but encounter is not done by me. '*You* encounters me by grace: it is not found by seeking ... *You* encounters me. But I enter into immediate relation with it.'[6]

You-relation, Buber writes elsewhere,[7] is the very 'cradle of real life'. And what is 'real life'? All real life is encounter.[8] Is life unreal, then, unless blessed with the occasional favour of encounter? This is hardly in line with Buber's other sayings and with his representation of the teachings of Hasidism and the sanctification of everyday life. On the other hand, history shows that it is out of *I-you* and *I-You* encounter that the truly creative, redemptive and revelatory acts draw their being. It is both from the mighty encounters, and from the little encounters between *I* and *you* and *You* that new creations, new redemptions and new revelations spring.

Where do relation and encounter occur?

Buber's three realms are a speciality of the Buberian life of dialogue, and an advance, some may feel, on the conventional preachments of religion which largely limit them to two: man/man and man/God.

The first is that of nature, animate and inanimate, the world of beasts, plants, rocks and elements. Here relation, not with nature as a whole as in some sort of mystical rapport, but individually with an exclusive *you*, is expressed below the level of speech. I say *you* to a tree by being wholly present with it and allowing it to be wholly present to me.

Needless to say, there has been argument about whether Buber was justified in including this field in his range of possible relation, especially since, according to him, relation must be reciprocated. As far as animals are concerned, it is apparent that on their own humble level they can affect the *I* and be affected by it. Enlarging on this subject in his postscript to the second edition of *I and Thou*, doubtless in response to queries and objections, Buber asserts that animals do not have a dual *I-you/I-it* nature, though they can consider things objectively as well as turn to other living beings in *I-you* relation. But when all is said and done, reciprocity in this context must remain a mystery. He adds, however, that those who show potential partnership with animals are not predominantly animal but predominantly spiritual by nature.

But what about plant life, not to mention inanimate matter? Corroborative evidence has been produced, which can of course be either accepted or discarded, suggesting that in the vegetable world there is more sensitivity than might be expected. Reciprocity of *you*-relation is to be seen, according to this theory, in the health and growth of the plants concerned.[9] But Buber himself lamented that so much can never break through the 'crust of thingness'. To his great regret, one of his most important intuitions, namely that there is no *I* in itself, but only *I-you* and *I-it*, did not occur between himself and the piece of quartz he was at the time holding in his hand, but in himself alone.

Of the creative, revelatory and redemptive forces in *I-you* relation and encounter with nature, little needs to be said. Everything, everywhere is a potential channel of them all.

The second realm of potential relation is the more familiar one of the interhuman. Here, it is expressed and returned in the form of speech. When I confront a human being as my *you*,

> and say to him the basic word *I-you*, he is neither a thing among things nor composed of things. He is not a *he* or a

44

she among neighbouring *he*s and *she*s, a point inscribed in a world-grid of space and time. He is not a character to be described and experienced, a loose bundle of named idiosyncrasies. Distinct and all of a piece, he is *you* and he fills the heavens. Not as though nothing exists apart from him, but all else lives in *his* light.[10]

Or I can move back from him to estimate qualities and failings, to place him in this or that context, or to assess his usefulness to me. He is in that case an *it* for me. I experience him from the distance of irrelation. I am not present with him.

In this human setting, it becomes plain that what is at work in the stand of *I-you*, in every sphere of relation, is essentially love. Love, Buber writes, is to be distinguished from feelings of love. Love is a position that I take up; feelings are what I have. Feelings reside in me; I reside in my love. Love is between *I* and *you*; it is not an emotion directed by an *I*-subject towards a *you*-object. To one who takes his stand in love,

> people become loosed from their involvement in the hustle and bustle of life. Good and bad, clever and silly, beautiful and ugly, one after another, they become real to him and *you* ... Love is the responsibility of an *I* for a *you*. Herein lies the similarity, not to be found in any feeling, between all who love, from the humblest to the greatest, from the blessedly protected whose life is completed in that of a single beloved person, to him who, nailed life-long to the cross of the world, dares that monstrous thing—to love all men.[11]

The realm of the third sphere of relation, where response takes the form of deed, is that of the *geistige Wesenheiten*. It is less easy to grasp, partly because of the variety of ways in which this term has been rendered in English, and partly because the subject is among the least well developed by commentators. Sometimes *geistige Wesenheiten* has been rendered as 'intelligible forms' (Ronald Gregor Smith, first version); sometimes as 'spiritual beings' (Smith, second version, and Kaufmann). Sometimes it appears as 'intelligible essences' (Friedman), or 'forms of the spirit' or simply 'forms' (R. E. Wood). One or two of these are more acceptable than the others, but none is exactly right. We will use here 'intellectual essences', because what Buber has in mind are the essence of art, knowledge and example, both that which is already in the world in the shape of visible works of art and scholarship and exemplary persons, and that which is still in the outer spaces of 'the genesis of word and form'. The latter one might define as ideas, but Buber considered the word 'idea' too passive for what he envisaged as vibrant 'beings', living and cruising about beyond man's consciousness, actively seeking an encounter which will redeem them from their exile and bring them to reality in the world.

Thus art, in a formula which must have pleased him since he repeats it at least twice, is 'work and witness to relation between *substantia humana* and *substantia rerum*', between human substance and the substance of things.[12] A poem, picture or musical composition does not arise from the artist's own soul. It springs from encounter between his *I* and an intellectual essence to which he says *you*. It is open to him to do nothing further; but he can be so gripped by his encounter that he commits himself wholly to it, through his own presence with it and its presence with him, to doing justice to the demands it makes of him. Then, having obtained reality in this way, and the consequent status of an *it*, the work of art that he produces will await futher encounters so that it can become the *you* of yet other *I*s.

In the case of the *geistige Wesenheit* of knowledge, *you*-response is made by way of the intellect itself. A thinker encounters an idea not yet brought into the world and converted into figures or words, and he gives himself over to realizing it. Banished into the 'thingness' of a mathematical formula or a literary work, the erstwhile *you* must next wait for redemption via a new encounter and another *I*.

With the third intellectual essence, defined by Buber as the example of 'pure action, action without arbitrariness'[13] we pass to another level entirely. While insisting that this is incomparably superior to the others, Buber has once more not made himself over-clear, but the theory as we understand it is that in the same way that the essences of art and knowledge await relation and encounter within and without the world, so does the spirit of 'pure action' wander among us inviting response, the example of living exemplary men and women, and of the holy dead known through their life and teachings. Kees Waaijman, a Dutch Carmelite,[14] concludes from what Buber writes that he supposed a preliminary response on the part of the exemplary one himself to his everlasting *You*, made through the medium of his existence. It is as a second stage that *I* enter into relation with that life as my *you* and express a response to it through the deeds of my own life.

In all of these three spheres of relation as laid out in *I and Thou*, I say *you* only with the whole of myself. Yet I cannot become whole solely through my own efforts. 'I become through *you*. Becoming *I*, I say *you*. All real life is encounter.'[15] I become wholly *me* through *you*-relation, and as I do so, my capacity for relation grows correspondingly.

Now this relation can be resolved into *I* and *you*, but it does not originate from their juxtaposition. *You* comes before the *I*. Irrelation, on the contrary, is post-*I*. Take the human infant. It is not true that a baby is first aware of an object as separate from itself and afterwards establishes relation with it. 'The struggle for relation, the cupped hand into which the vis-à-vis nestles, comes first. Relation to it, a wordless pre-form saying of *you*, comes second.'[16]

In the beginning is relation. But the *a priori* of relation is the inborn *you*, inborn because in the womb the child is enfolded in natural relation, the bonds of which are broken at birth. It then has to realize the inborn *you* in what it meets in the world in which it newly finds itself. Giving cosmic and metacosmic roots to the longing for relation, Buber believed that this reaches back into a primordial world from which, although already born, the baby still has to emerge through its own efforts. 'Man', he repeats, 'becomes *I* through *you*'.[17] Whereas at first the *I* is merely something which reaches out towards *you*, eventually the link breaks and, after briefly confronting itself as a *you*, it enters into relation in full self-awareness. It is also then ready to adopt the stand of detachment known as *I-it*.

Part Two of *I and Thou* deals mainly with the world of *it* and the damage caused when detachment takes precedence over *I-you* relation.

Our basic commerce with life from the standpoint *I-it* is experience, which increases the substance of *it*, and use, which applies *it* to its ends, i.e. the preservation, relief and provisioning of human existence. This world of irrelation is growing; our ability to experience and use is becoming more and more expert and our capacity for relation—by virtue of which alone we are able to live in the spirit—is diminishing.

What is spirit? In its human manifestation, it is the human response to a *you*. It does not reside in the *I* but between *I* and *you*. I live in the spirit as long as I can say *you* in the three spheres of relation.

One who takes his stand mainly in irrelation, divides his life between the neatly separate preserves of institutions and feelings. Institutions are where he transacts his business, negotiates among other human heads and limbs, and works; and feelings are where he recovers from all this, where he 'indulges his affection, hatred, pleasure and, as long as it is not too sharp, his pain'.[18] Neither institutions nor feelings know anything of presence, either the presence of people, or even of present time. For present time exists only where the presence of relation and encounter exist and occur. Feelings, for their part, know only the hurrying moment, the not-yet.

It has been suggested that if institutions do not conduce to public life they should be injected with feelings. The State, for instance, should be replaced by a community of love. But true community arises, not from people having feelings about one another, but firstly from

> their all being in living reciprocal relation with one another. The second derives from the first but is not given with the first alone. Living reciprocal relation includes feelings but does not spring from them. Community is built from living reciprocal relation; but the builder is the living operative Centre.[19]

The same applies to institutions of the private life such as

marriage. Marriage cannot be renewed from feelings, nor
without them of course. But the one source from which it can
be renewed is when 'two people reveal *you* to one another'.[20]
And again, as in the large community, it is a central Presence
which ultimately makes for human life, 'the third element, the
central presence of *You*. Or more exactly, the central *You*
perceived in the present'.[21]

Human life cannot dispense with distance and objectivity, as
has already been said—as long as present relation is never far off.
There is nothing wrong in desiring profit or power—as long as
it is joined to a desire for the nearness and reciprocity of relation.
But the businessman or statesman obedient to the spirit is not a
fanatic. He knows that he cannot treat as *you* everyone with
whom he has to deal. He does so simply as far as he is able. For
the problem of real life it is important whether or not

> spirit, the *you*-saying and *you*-responding spirit, remains in
> life and reality; whether that of it which is still to be found
> in public life becomes further subject to the State and the
> economy or independently effective; whether that of it
> which still lingers in human, personal life becomes part of
> public life: this is decisive.[22]

Such a state of affairs will not come about by dividing life into
spirit and secular, two separate compartments. Spirit's task is to
redeem the world, and this, 'the dissipated, feeble, degenerate
spirituality which passes for spirit today can only do by
attaining once more to the essence of spirit: the ability to say
you.'[23]

There follows a short exploration of freedom and destiny in
human life. In the world of experience and use, all seems to be
either caused or causative. Yet causality, which is of the utmost
significance to science, need not depress those who can leave
that world for the world of *you*. There, the reciprocity of *I* and
you is unaffected by it, and people decide on their own right
action and know that they are free. They know that it is a
natural part of life to swing from relation to the absence of it,
and they are not worried. They are content to set their foot on
the threshold on which they may not stay, and even recognize

that it is part and parcel of the meaning and destiny of life that they have repeatedly to leave it. Destiny goes hand in hand with freedom. Indeed, to one who sets aside 'goods and garments' and 'stands naked before the Face', destiny appears as the counterpart of freedom.

Every great civilization has its beginnings in an original relational event, an essential act of the spirit, a response to *You*. But the freedom and creativity inspired by it last only as long as that relation is repeated in the life of the individual. Once a civilization ceases to be centred on that same endlessly repeated act, it stiffens into a world caught in the grip of fate. In the twentieth century, belief in fate is more entrenched than ever before. There is a law of survival, according to which all must struggle to survive; a psychological law, which lays down that the personality is formed of inborn natural instincts; a law of civilization, which ordains the inevitable and uniform genesis and decline of historical structures. There seems to be no room for freedom, no way out. And yet, in the sickness of our own civilization, which is unlike all the others yet part of them, a nameless path runs down to a spiritual underworld where there is neither forwards nor backwards, but only the turning, *teshuvah*. Nothing can become fate except belief in fate— because it suppresses the movement of *teshuvah*.

But how can an *I* which has become unreal through constant commerce with the world of experience and use summon up the power to recognize the world for what it is? If a man lives arbitrarily, how can be become aware that he is free?

The free decide and choose without arbitrariness. They believe in destiny and that it needs them. They look and listen for it. They sacrifice their unfree lesser will for the greater one. They watch for what develops so that they can help to give it reality through human spirit, human life and human death. They believe. To live arbitrarily is to live without belief or encounter and to be concerned merely to exploit a situation to one's advantage. For such a one, existence is merely a business of fixing aims and devising the means to attain them.

Without sacrifice and without grace, without encounter

and without presence, his world is a world of ends and means. It cannot be otherwise. And this is called fate. Thus in all his arbitrariness he is inextricably caught up in unreality. And he knows it whenever he reflects on himself.[24]

He therefore takes care not to do so. But if he would allow himself to meditate on the real *I* and the unreal *I*, and let himself if necessary sink into the depths of despair, this would be the beginning of his *teshuvah*.

While I experience and use, my *I* is an egotist. In the stand of relation, my *I* is a person. The egotist makes its appearance in setting itself off against other egotists. The person makes its appearance by entering into relation with other persons. These are two poles rather than two human types, for no one is purely egotist and no one purely person. 'None is wholly real and none is wholly unreal. All live in a dual *I*.'[25] Yet some are so distinctly egotist that they may be called egotists, and some so distinctly person that they may be called persons.

The third and last part of *I and Thou* is devoted to relation between the *I* and its everlasting *You*. Sometimes this is almost pantheistically identified with *I-you* relation (with the small *you*). For instance, of relation with nature, Maurice Friedman maintains: 'This meeting with the Thou of man and nature is also a meeting with God.'[26] But what Buber actually writes is that the parallel lines of relation come together in the everlasting *You* and that with each *you* we catch a *glimpse* of the everlasting one. With each finite *you* we look towards the 'hem' of the garment of the everlasting *You*.

> With every particular *you*, the basic word *I-you* addresses the everlasting *You*. From this mediation of the *you* of all beings, fulfilment of relation comes to them and unfulfilment. The inborn *you* is realized in each but perfected in none. It is perfected only in immediate relation with that *You* which cannot by nature become an *it*.[27]

The everlasting *You* has been given many names, but

eventually they have become part of the language of the *it*-world in which God is the object of speculation and thought. It is therefore sometimes felt that the word 'God' should be avoided because it has been misused. But what does it matter that so many mistakes have been committed in regard to his being and actions beside the fact that by 'God' people have addressed their everlasting *You*?

To enter into and maintain perfect relation, a person must first have become one and whole through other *you*-relation. He must have become a unified human being in whom nothing isolated stirs any more, nothing partial. He must be one for whom whatever is done is done with the whole of himself. To have won stability in such a condition is to be able to go out towards 'supreme encounter'.

For this, there is no need of special instruction or exercises. 'Nothing of anything that has been contrived or devised through the ages of the human spirit by way of instruction, preparation, training or meditation has to do with the most simple fact of encounter.'[28] None of this leads anywhere except to the *it*-world. All that is needed is a total acceptance of Presence and presence in the present time. But the deeper the alienation from relation in and with the world the more radical will such a *teshuvah* be.

Immediate relation in the world is exclusive: but perfect relation is simultaneously absolutely exclusive and absolutely inclusive. It does not demand that one averts the eyes from all else, but to see all else in an ever-present Vis-à-Vis. 'We do not find God by remaining in the world. We do not find God by leaving the world. He finds him who is not to be sought who goes out towards his *You* with his whole being, bearing with him the whole being of the world.'[29]

The essential element of relation with God is not to be reduced to a feeling, and specifically a feeling of dependence. Dependence is certainly felt; but so is freedom. We need God; but God also needs us. Creation happens to us and we tremble and submit; but also 'we take part in it; we encounter the Creator (*dem Schaffenden*); we reach out to him as helpers and associates'.[30] To reduce perfect relation to dependence is to deprive both partners, and with them relation itself, of reality.

The same happens if the essential element of relation with *You* is thought to be a turning inward into the self, either by ridding it of the *I*, or by imagining that the self is alone, that which thinks and is. In the first case, it is thought that God enters the *I*-less being and merges with it, as in the saying of the evangelist John, 'I and the Father are one.' The second, the teaching of Shandilya, a medieval Hindu theist, supposes that 'The All-embracing is my Self in my inmost heart', and identifies *I* and *You*. In both cases, the act of relation is abolished, in the first because one partner swallows up the other, and in the second because the duality of *I* and *You* is actually denied. But in lived reality there is no unity of being. There is only a unification of the *I*, the gathering of its powers into one. For whereas the doctrine of immersion within the self asks for the preservation only of what is pure, true unification 'esteems the instinctive not too impure, the sensual not too peripheral, the emotional not too transient.'[31]

Buddha, the perfect one who makes perfect, declined to assert that there is or is not unity. He desired to teach the Way, not an opinion. He disputed one statement only: that there is no doing, no deed, no power. And he made one assertion only: 'There is, O monks, an unbecome, an uncreated, an un-formed.'[32] Otherwise, there would be no goal to the Way. But we know, says Buber, that if this is one of the goals, it cannot be ours; and if it is the goal, it is wrongly described. Buddha leads to one goal that is ours, the unification of the soul; but even this is by means of turning away from the 'deception of form', which is for us no deception but the world. Furthermore, Buddha's teaching points away from relation altogether.

All teaching of immersion within the self is based on the gigantic illusion of man turned back on himself that spirit is in him, whereas it is *between* himself and what is not himself. Also, if I merely redeem myself in the world, I do the world neither good nor ill. To affect it, I must believe in it; and if I do this, I cannot be Godless. 'Whoever truly goes out to the world, goes out to God.'[33]

Man's religious situation, his 'existence (*Dasein*) in the Presence',[34] is characterized by the essential paradox that everything is entirely out of his hands and yet depends on him. The paradox is insoluble. It cannot be tampered with, synthesized or relativized. No theological artifice can be allowed to provide an abstract reconciliation between thesis and antithesis. The significance of the religious situation is that the paradox has to be lived. But in the reality of a life of standing-before-God, necessity and freedom are seen to be one.

All relation in the world is alternatively actual and latent. Only the everlasting *You* is by nature everlastingly *You*. It is our nature which obliges us to draw it into the world and language of *it*.

The world of irrelation coheres in a context of space and time. The world of relation coheres in neither. It coheres at its Centre, in the everlasting *You* in which the parallel lines of other relation meet. Perfect relation between *I* and *You* provides a *you*-continuum which ensures that individual moments of relation combine to form a life of relation. Also, perfect relation lends to other relation formative powers which are able to penetrate and change the world of experience and use. This turning back to perfect relation, this *teshuvah*, is a re-recognition of the Centre. In this act of our being, our capacity for relation acquires new life, and in so doing renews the life of the world.

With every *you*, we look towards the hem of the everlasting *You*. We hear the everlasting *You* breathing in every one. Every *you* is a gateway to the Presence of the Word. But when perfect encounter takes place, the gateways come together to form One Portal into real life, and we no longer know by which gate we have entered.

As for solitude being a way to the Mystery, we can even become so infatuated with ourselves as to imagine that God is in us and that we speak to him. 'But however true it is that God encompasses us and dwells in us, we never have him in us. And we speak with him only when speech within us has come to an end.'[35]

It has been said that we either believe in God, or in an idol such as money, sex or power, and that we only have to realize that the idols are no more than relative goods for the religious act to be diverted to its proper end. But this is to place relationship with an idol on the same footing as relation with *You*. How can anyone turn back to relation with *You*, make his *teshuvah*, when relation itself is unknown to him? A servant of Mammon cannot say *you* to money. Whoever substitutes God for his idol, 'has' a phantom to which he gives the name of God. 'But God, the everlasting Presence, does not permit himself to be "had". Woe to the possessed who thinks he possesses God!'[36]

Some speak of the religious man as one who can do without relation other than that with God. They think of him as having outstripped 'social' man. But social existence can mean two things. It can mean community built on relation, a product of the same energy as that which operates between man and God, or it can mean the massing together of people in conditions empty of relation. Now a person cannot divide his life between real relation with God and unreal relationship with the world. Whoever envisages the world as an object of experience and use, does the same to God. He prays to unburden himself and his prayer falls into the ear of the void. It is he who is Godless, not the unbeliever who calls on the Nameless One out of his darkness and longing.

Again, some say that the religious man has outdistanced moral man with his obligations towards the world. He has left behind the tension between the right and wrong and is involved instead as a single isolated being in a tension between the world and God where he is commanded to divest himself of demands and responsibilities. What he does in the world counts for nothing. But the truth is that for whoever approaches the Presence, the world itself becomes so fully present that he can with one word say *you* to the being of all beings.

Moral judgement of others is finished with forever, but his own right action is weighed up constantly. What he does in the world is then not valueless but 'intended, asked for, needed and part of creation'.[37]

Now follows the significant adjustment which Buber inserted into the revised edition of *Ich und Du*. The reason for the change will be discussed in greater detail later, in connection with the Buber–Rosenzweig Bible translation, but for the moment all that needs to be said is that it occurs in the phrase in which God alludes to himself on Sinai in Exodus 3:14 in the story of the burning bush. What shall I say to the Israelites, Moses asks God, when they enquire about your Name? 'I am that I am', is the cryptic reply placed in God's mouth by his interpreters and translators, and this is how Buber gives it in the 1923 first edition. This, too, is how it appears, as has been said, in Ronald Gregor Smith's English translation. Between 1923 and 1926, however, Buber had worked with Franz Rosenzweig on the translation of Exodus from the Hebrew into German[38] and between them they had come to the conclusion that this 'I am that I am' is not the meaning intended in the original. They perceived in the phrase a notion of presence. Instead, therefore, they translated God's words as, 'I will be there such as I will be there' (or 'I am there such as I am there', the English present or future tense being covered by the imperfect one in Hebrew). With this apparently small but crucial alteration, Buber in fact brought to his theme of 'religion as presence'—for the course given in 1922 in the Frankfurt Lehrhaus was clearly a run-in of *Ich und Du*—the one essential element it lacked: biblical backing for his everlasting *You*.

The eternal and primordial phenomenon of what is known as revelation is that one does not come out of supreme encounter the same as one entered it. Something is added. Presence is given in the form of strength.

This Presence as strength comprises three effects. The first is that one is aware of being bound in relation without knowing to what, or how, and without life being lightened in any way: on the contrary, it becomes heavier with meaning. Secondly, this meaning is sure: nothing can ever again be meaningless. And it is a meaning that has to be done, not expounded. Thirdly, it is a meaning that concerns this present life and world and not another; it must be substantiated through unity of being and unity of existence.

As no teaching or instruction can lead to encounter with *You*, so none can lead out of it. We reach it simply by saying *You*, and we leave it by saying *You*.

> That before which, within which, out of which and into which we live, the Mystery, remains what it was. It has become present to us and with its presence declared itself to be salvation. We have 'known' it, but have no knowledge of it that might lessen or moderate its mysteriousness. We have drawn near to God, but no nearer to any unravelling or unveiling of existence. We have sensed redemption (*Erlösung*) but no solution (*Lösung*), we cannot go to others with what we have received and say, 'This is what you should know; this is what should be done.' We can only go and prove it to be true. And even this is no 'should'. We can and we must. This is the everlasting revelation present in the here and now. I know of none whose primordial phenomenon is not the same. I believe in none. I believe in no self-naming of God, in no self-defining of God before men. The word of revelation is, *I am there such as I am there*. That which reveals is that which reveals. That which is, is there. Nothing more. The everlasting source of strength flows on. The everlasting voice sounds. Nothing more.[39]

Why is it that presence and strength of revelation—for all religions have their origin in some kind of revelation—change into knowledge pronounced and promulgated, and a code of behaviour laid down?

The answer is that man longs to have God continuously in time and space, and this longing is not satisfied by perfect relation. Not content with the alternate latency and actuality of the human ability to say *you*, he therefore makes God into an object of faith. He prefers the duration of an *it* believed in, and the security it offers *because* of his belief, to the insecurity of relation with *You*. Similarly, he wishes to extend God-having in space. He wants a community of the faithful united with their

God. He consequently makes God into an object of worship, which begins by supplementing his relation with *You* but ultimately tends to supplant it.

Temporal continuity of *you*-relation can, however, only be ensured by realizing the everlasting *You* in the world. Likewise, spatial continuity of *You*-relation can only be ensured by being bound to others, not in order to participate in a central *You*, but *because* each individually is bound to a central *You*.

The purpose of encounter with *You* is not that we should concern ourselves with God, but that we should corroborate to the world the meaning we have perceived. By bending back towards God, we turn away from him. No *You* confronts us any more. We can then only instal God in thingness as an *it*, and believe in him and talk about him as an *it*. For what seems to be a turning *towards* the First Cause is in fact part of a metacosmic movement *away* from it. And what seems a turning *away* from God on the part of one who fulfils his mission in the world is in fact part of a metacosmic movement *towards* him.

These two movements—a turning away into growth and expansion and a turning back towards relation—find their supreme form in the history of human relation to God. In *teshuvah*, the Word—by which Buber presumably means *I-You*—is born on earth. As it grows and expands, it changes into the chrysalis of religion. In a new *teshuvah* it acquires new wings.

Throughout the ages, fresh material from the world of the spirit is continuously lifted up and shaped into a form of God, whom we never see without the world but only the world in him. These forms are a mixture of *You* and *it*. In religion and worship, they can stiffen into an object and yet become present because of the essence of relation still alive in them. But prayer can degenerate to the extent that it becomes more and more difficult for the whole and undivided *I* to say and pray *You*. When that happens, a person must leave the false security of religion and make for the hazards of the infinite. 'From a community whose roof is the Dome of the Temple but not the sky, he must go out into final solitude.'[40] When religion's movement towards its own growth suppresses the movement towards relation known as *teshuvah*, the form of God that it promulgates dies, and all that has been built around it collapses in ruins. 'And it is part of what happens there that in the dislocation of his truth man no longer sees what happens there. What happens is the decomposition of the Word.'[41] The Word has its essence in revelation; is active while the divine form lives; and becomes mere currency during the dominion of the dead form. But the course is not circular. It is the Way. And with each age, fate becomes more oppressive and our *teshuvah* more explosive.

> History is a mysterious approach. Every twist of its way leads at once into deeper corruption and a more fundamental *teshuvah*. But the phenomenon known in its worldly aspect as *teshuvah* has a divine aspect known as redemption.[42]

Thus, in summary, the 'little book' *I and Thou* begins with an overview of the alternatives of dialogue and its absence in everyday life, entering more carefully into the *I* of its stand of *I-you* relation. It next moves into the world of *it*, to which so much is owed by way of knowledge and even survival itself, discussing the real *I* of dialogue and the unreal *I* of experience and use. It introduces also the notion of the everlasting *You* and the concept of *teshuvah*. Lastly, it sees the human *I* unified and made real through relation in and with the world, become at last fully whole through *teshuvah*, whereby it moves into the religious situation of 'existence in the Presence', with all the necessary response and responsibilities which that engagement demands.

5

THE HEBREW BIBLE

When in 1925 Buber accepted the invitation of the publisher Lambert Schneider to undertake a new German translation of the Bible, he was forty-seven years old; he cannot have foreseen that he was embracing a task which would occupy him, with interruptions, until he was well in his eighties. He complied on condition that Franz Rosenzweig joined him as collaborator. By that time gravely ill and confined to his home, Rosenzweig had in the past consulted him in his own work of translating the poems of Judah Halevi. The co-operation was agreed to after a few false starts—Rosenzweig thought it preferable to revise the Luther text, whereas Buber was for a totally fresh and unrestricted version direct from the original—the two men were soon busy with the book of Genesis. Buber translated, and despatched the resulting batches of paper to Rosenzweig, mostly in chapters, and the latter sent back comments and suggestions which were weighed up by Buber and incorporated or not as the case might be. Further correspondence dealt with any material not accepted in this way, and whatever was still unsettled was discussed during the weekly Wednesday visits when Buber taught in the mornings in Frankfurt and spent the rest of the day with his friend. Communication between the two had by then to be carried on with the help of an alphabet apparatus to which Rosenzweig pointed with one finger, and with the assistance of his wife, Edith.

In Buber's view, the various versions had transformed the Bible into a palimpsest. The ancient words had become overlaid with a veneer 'partly theological and partly literary in origin'[1] which had to be cleared away for their true significance to be rediscovered. In addition, great efforts had to be made to recapture the 'spokenness' (*Gesprochenheit*) of the Bible. For generations it had been handed down orally, not only the psalms and the proverbs, but also the law and the narrative portions. In his account of the work carried out at first by himself and Rosenzweig, and afterwards by himself alone, Buber writes that God did not tell Joshua not to allow the Torah to leave his eyes, but his 'mouth'. If the new German version were likewise to be suitable for oral recitation, attention had to be paid to remaining close to the Hebrew sentence forms, to rendering words near to one another in meaning but separated in the text, by related verbal roots or similar-sounding words, and to following the Hebrew rhythm. Only so would its unfamiliarity not degenerate into strangeness, though the unfamiliarity was itself necessary if there were to be any sort of encounter between the biblical text and contemporary man. The aim was to retain and communicate the written material as it is, for after all, unlike a commentary, a translation must actually take the place of the original.

Another principle following from the attempt to reproduce a text intended to be read aloud was that it should be divided into 'breath measures'. No sentence, that is to say, was to be so long as to require a fresh inhalation on the part of the reader.

As it is not easy to convey *in vacuo* the qualities of a translation from one foreign tongue to another, a brief example of the rendering of the Buber/Rosenzweig rendering of a familiar text, Genesis 2:4–8, may be helpful. The Revised Standard Version reads:

> In the day that the LORD God made the earth and the heavens, when no plant of the field was yet in the earth and no herb of the field had yet sprung up—for the LORD God had not caused it to rain upon the earth, and there was no man to till the ground; but a mist went up from the earth and watered the whole face of the ground—then the LORD God formed man of dust from the ground, and breathed into his nostrils the breath of life; and man became a living being.

This becomes in Buber's and Rosenzweig's hands:

On the day that HE, God, made earth and heaven, every
bush of the field was not yet on the earth, every plant was
not yet sprung up, for HE, God, had not caused it to rain
over the earth, and there was no man, Adam, to attend to
the soil, Adama: out of the earth rose a vapour and
moistened all the face of the soil, and HE, God, formed
man, dust from the soil, and blew into his nostrils breath
of life, and man became a living being.

When Rosenzweig, who had been doubtful about the whole
enterprise, saw Buber's first sample, he was amazed. The patina
has gone, he exclaimed. The text was now as good as new, and
that must be a good thing. He was won over.

The resulting *Die Schrift* is generally held to be remarkable.
In Hans Kohn's opinion, 'it cuts an underground passage from
the original to the language of the translation. It does not render
something found into something found, but wrestles conscien-
tiously with the German language to its uttermost possibilities'.[2]
It fully reproduces the Hebrew, Kohn thought, and by remaining so faithful, throws light on profound meaning.

Needless to say, not everyone likes it. The strangeness itself,
which the translators deliberately contrived by forcing German
into odd shapes and into new words and sounds, causes unease.
For instance, the Hebrew *ruaḥ* means both wind (*Wind*) and
spirit (*Geist*). Buber and Rosenzweig felt that *Geist* had lost the
dynamism it once possessed, so they substituted for it *Braus*,
from *brausen*, to rush, to effervesce, to surge, dividing this again
into *Windbraus* and *Geistbraus*. So when in the text there is
question of spirit as an electric creative force, the word used is
Geistbraus; where the allusion is to a natural event but one
caused from above, the word chosen is *Windbraus*; and where
wind pure and simple is meant, *ruaḥ* is translated as plain *Wind*.

All in all, it is a very different Bible from any that had gone
before and Buber and Rosenzweig guessed that it would not
find general favour. But as Rosenzweig wrote to his colleague
in August 1926, they were faced with two kinds of readers:
those who know nothing and those who know everything. If
the translators did their work properly, the first would

understand everything, and the rest nothing at all. The first would believe that what Buber and Rosenzweig had written, and what they themselves had understood, was what was meant. The others would be mistrustful. They would think that what was there, and what they understood it to mean, was not what was meant. So they would 'compare' it. If they compared it with the original Hebrew text, they would join the first party, which would thereby increase from one to about eleven per cent. But those who compared it with the German Lutheran text would be lost. 'The one per cent understand immediately what is meant by *Braus*... the ten per cent never, for they look for a translation of *Geist*... and there they can admittedly look for a long time.'[3]

In September 1927, Rosenzweig was again expressing his opinion of their achievement:

> Someone expecting a work of art *cannot* understand us. Yet it is one. But visible as such only to one not looking for it. In the same way that the elegance of a mathematical proof is apparent only to those who approach it with mathematical interests and not searching for elegance.[4]

Alfred Jeremias, the Lutheran theologian and Assyriologist, greatly admired it. He studied fascicles 1–5 with 'burning interest' and was convinced that the new Bible would become the number one translation for German Jews.

Franz Rosenzweig's sufferings ended with his death in 1929, by which time he and Buber had reached the Book of Isaiah. From then on, Buber continued the work alone until 1932, then laid it aside until 1949. The final volume of the revised *Die Schrift* was not published until 1961.

It should be mentioned before turning to the first of the works stimulated by his study of the biblical text that Buber was already thinking in the twenties of emigrating to Palestine. But he decided against it. 'I cannot,' he told Hans Kohn in a letter, 'Hebraize myself in the sense of productivity and must content myself with living and dying as a frontier guard.'[5]

Kingship of God, published in 1932 and already sold out by the beginning of 1934, is a book of 222 pages, 158 of which are devoted to notes. An exegetical work proper, more scholarly in presentation than his later *Moses* and *The Prophetic Faith*, it was intended to be part of a larger work enquiring into the origin of messianism in Israel, a problem with which Buber had concerned himself, and on which he had frequently lectured, during the preceding seven years. He had meant to follow the relationship between God and Israel as it developed through the ages and to demonstrate how the notion came into being of a human king who would be the follower of YHWH the King, his anointed one, his messiah, his *christos kyriou*. In fact Buber managed to get no further than an investigation into YHWH the King in the present volume and, in a further shorter piece,[6] to the anointing of Saul by Samuel.

Beginning with the story of Gideon, who refused after his victory over Midian to accept the invitation of the men of Israel to rule over them, saying, 'Not I shall rule over you/ nor shall my son rule over you/ HE shall rule over you', Buber sets out to show in this book how real to ancient Israel was the concept of their God as a deity who essentially walked before them, dwelt among them, guided them and sustained them. YHWH ruled over them directly, as a people and also as individuals. He was a God of action and movement. He was a living Presence. In this connection, Buber for the first time discusses the rendering of the Bible translation of the saying by God to Moses on Sinai, *ehyeh asher ehyeh*. Normally given as 'I am that I am', the Buber / Rosenzweig version reads, as has been said, 'I am there such as I am there', *(ich bin da als der ich da bin)*. The justification for this reading of Exodus 3 : 14, which is entered into in greater detail later in the summary of *Moses* (as is the use of the pronoun in capital letters for the Name of God), did not convince Gershom Scholem for one. Buber should have explained himself at greater length, he said. 'You are right,' was Buber's reply, 'but as far as the decisive issue was concerned, I thought I could confine myself to pointing to Rosenzweig, from whom came the encouragement and to my mind the highly important interpretation, *asher* = such as.'[7]

'Burning interest' was at all events shown once again when *Kingship of God* came out, this time by the Swiss theologian Emil Brunner. At last! at last! he jubilated, a book on an Old Testament theme written with understanding instead of mis-understanding.

With the rise of National Socialism, Buber was in 1933 forced to resign his university chair. The question of his emigration to Palestine still hung in the air, despite his belief that he would be unable to 'Hebraize' himself, and in the four years between the appearance of *Kingship of God* and the next publication of note, the very different *Question to the Single One*, much correspond-ence travelled between Heppenheim an der Bergstrasse, where the Bubers lived, and Gershom Scholem in Jerusalem. The latter sincerely wanted Buber, as a person of standing and authority, to join the Hebrew University, and in February 1934 was even able to tell him that an application had been made to Council to establish a chair of general religious studies and to call on him to occupy it. The matter, it seemed, was at last under way. Within a fortnight, another letter reached him from Scholem, still sanguine and telling Buber that he might soon hear from Judah Magnes, the Chancellor of the University. It was now for Buber to make up his mind whether to travel to Jerusalem that winter. In the event, Magnes did confirm the invitation but Buber's reaction was not over-eager. He acknowledged the letter and said he would consider it, but he was clearly not impressed by the terms of the appointment, which were for two years' tenure on a higher salary or a five-year tenure on a lower one. As it happened, by the end of the summer the affair was out of his hands.

Magnes had had to explain that the project had fallen through. 'For the problem of Jewish religion,' he told Buber, 'the subject is not suitable or necessary, and for the subject, a brilliant writer is not enough of a scholar.'[8] Buber's observation apropos of this was that he did not understand the first point, and the second seemed to overlook his academic activity in the University of Frankfurt. 'All in all, one more experience'[9] was his laconic comment.

Meanwhile, Buber was deeply preoccupied with the political situation at home. Before 1933, his impact on German Jewry had been powerful but not very widespread, but in the work which he took upon himself from then on until he left the country five years later, he made himself very well known and almost indispensable to them. Primarily, he became responsible, first, for drafting plans for the body representing the Jews in Germany (*Reichsvertretung der deutschen Juden*) for the foundation of a Central Office for Jewish Adult Education (*Mittelstelle für jüdische Erwachsenenbildung*), and second, for taking over the direction of that Office. Its aim, so it was decided, should be to promote the exchange of ideas between institutions concerned with adult education in Germany, to stimulate the formation of new ones, to reorganize those in existence so that they corresponded to a need, and in all relevant questions to be at the disposition of organizations and individuals with help and advice. The *Mittelstelle* should in addition be available for the schools section of the *Reichsvertretung*, to co-operate with the further education of teachers. It was also to produce a periodical. Buber's feeling was that the great problem of the time was one of education, education for resistance, but also for preparing for a new life in Palestine. He convened a conference from 10–13 May 1934, which about sixty people attended, to discuss questions relating to adult education. Ranging in age from the twenties to the sixties, the participants included representatives of various callings: rabbis, teachers, officials of larger Jewish bodies, leaders of youth groups. The main teaching staff of the *Mittelstelle* was constituted, and by the last week in May the first three-day course took place at Bad Kreuznach.

At this time, Ernst Simon returned to Germany at Buber's request to join in the teaching programme of the *Mittelstelle*. Simon, who had been associated with the Lehrhaus in Frankfurt from 1920 until he left for Palestine in 1928, and had also co-edited *Der Jude* with Buber, proved of invaluable assistance during the eight months that he stayed. Soon after his arrival, he took over at the Bad Kreuznach event a seminar for Buber, who was ill, besides delivering two lectures, one on the significance of Palestine for Jewish education in Germany, the other on 'The prophet Jeremiah and his message to us', and he organized a seminar of his own on the sixteenth-century character Jossel of Rosheim. Other lecturers gave papers and held seminars on such subjects as Hebrew teaching methods, the function and tasks of the *Mittelstelle*, and work in smaller community groups.

Buber himself travelled from one end of Germany to another, conducting courses and giving lectures, mostly on biblical figures and topics. He soon gathered a substantial following, above all among those belonging to youth organizations, and often he was away for a week or more in some remote spot with one or other of these gatherings. At first everything went well and his arrangements were untroubled by the authorities, but in February 1935, after a talk given at the Lehrhaus in Frankfurt on 'The power of the spirit', he was barred from speaking in public and at Jewish meetings. In March, moreover, it turned out that this ban included teaching. However, after tedious negotiations, a limited amount of instruction was again allowed within the confines of the *Mittelstelle*. Circumstances nevertheless became more and more difficult from then on until 1938, when Buber left the country; though as Robert Weltsch writes,[10] during those five years an immense amount of good work had been done. Indeed, it can be claimed that the days of the *Mittelstelle* paved the way for a new concept of Jewish education and training, the impact of which is felt in many institutions in Israel but also in the Diaspora. 'Wherever Jewish training is carried out in the world today,' Weltsch asserts, 'the name of Buber cannot be ignored. Directly and indirectly, often watered down or misunderstood, the mighty stream which flowed from Buber's popular education also reached and fructified those which were far away.'[11]

In spite of the political pressures, Buber was for the time being still able to publish and 1936 saw the appearance of *The Question to the Single One*, which he describes in his foreword to the English edition[12] as the elaboration of an address given to the students of three German-Swiss universities at the close of 1933. The fact that it came out at all was, Buber says, astonishing 'because it attacks the life-basis of totalitarianism'. The reason must have been that it was not properly understood.

This short work considers the constitution and role, and enlarges on the concept introduced in *I and Thou*, of the unified and integrated 'person'. Kierkegaard's so-called 'single one' or individual (*der Einzelne*) around whom the argument turns, withdrawn from the world and from the woman he loved, Regina Olsen, and preoccupied with his torments and with his God, is predictably deplored. So is another human category, that of Max Stirner's 'unique one' (*der Einzige*), the 'free personality', also severed from the world, divorced from the otherness of things and people, which serve only to feed his own selfhood. As far as the 'individual' is concerned, the ideal according to Buber is not to be essentially involved with God and only relatively with others. The ideal is to be a 'person' for whom the reality of relation with God includes relation with all else. But at that time (the 1930s, that is), the 'person' was at risk, as was also truth. The 'person' was threatened by collectivization, truth by politicization. It was nevertheless imperative that 'persons' should continue, not merely as representatives elected to take over responsibility for others, but as men and women able to shoulder responsibility for themselves. Also, belief in truth was necessary as something independent of man, something impossible to hold within the self, but with which one might live in genuine relation.

'Individuals' must be responsible to the truth as it manifests itself in their historical situation. They must hold their own in the face of the whole of existence present to them, public life included. In fact, true community and true community life can only be real to the extent that 'individuals' comprising it become real, become 'persons' out of whose responsible personal life public life is renewed.

Albert Schweitzer, with whom Buber was in touch from 1928 until his old age, could not understand why he had bothered with Kierkegaard at all. Thanking him for a copy of *The Question to the Single One*, he asked Buber quite frankly:

Why do you take issue with this poor psychopath? He is no thinker. I read him only with aversion. What does he

actually want?... He has only been made into a thinker
by everything people have written about him.[13]

In Jerusalem, after yet another debate, the Senate decision to
appoint Buber this time to a chair of social philosophy was at
last ratified. He and Paula consequently travelled to Palestine in
May 1937 to look for somewhere to live. Back in Heppenheim
again, more exasperation awaited them in the form of delays
concerning work permits and the disposal of their property.
Also, Martin suffered another of his bouts of 'severe and
stubborn influenza' and Paula had the misfortune to fall down
the cellar steps and was unable to walk for a week. The direction
of the *Mittelstelle* was handed over to Ernst Kantorowicz.
Formerly a profesor at a Frankfurt teacher-training college, an
assimilated Jew to whom Jewish concerns, national and religious, had become quite foreign, he had developed into a
leading figure, with Buber, in the running of *Mittelstelle* affairs.
The Bubers left in March 1938. In May, Kantorowicz wrote to
say that the free seminars had fallen victim to the regime. Later,
he and his wife were expelled to Holland, from where he wrote
to ask Buber to look for employment for him, since he had no
permission to work in the Netherlands. But he was arrested
there in 1940 and died with his wife in Auschwitz.

Buber had intended to return to Germany, where they
counted on him for help in the educational field, but the
Kristallnacht outrage of 9–10 November caused him to change
his plans and he decided to stay in Jerusalem permanently. He
was sixty years old.

6

IN PALESTINE

Here everything is more alarming, more chaotic, more
cruel and more innocent than one can imagine. You
ought to come here some time. What is to be experienced
here of reality and of the Indwelling 'in the midst of our
stain' is probably to be experienced nowhere else.[1]

So wrote Buber in a letter of 1 August 1938 to his close friend
Hans Trüb (one of the very few whom he addressed as 'du'), a
psychoanalyst and psychotherapist of the school of Jung, from
whom under Buber's influence he later diverged. Palestine was
in fact in turmoil, with bloody attacks by Arab terrorists on the
one hand, and on the other fearsome reprisals on the part of the
Stern Gang and Irgun Zevai Leumi led by Menachem Begin.
Terror bred terror, though the Haganah, the Jewish self-defence
organization, held back from acts of revenge and the Jewish
Agency condemned them.

Nevertheless, as far as his work was concerned, it was not
long before Buber was in the grip of a lively surge of activity
which manifested itself over the following years in a series of
important publications. The uprooting from Germany and the
switch to another language had not been easy, and there had
been an earlier period of depression, but by 1945 he was in a
position to see the realization or partial realization of several
projects which had lain dormant for a long time. Also his
academic work, which had necessarily called for much preparation, was going well and without stress. Paula, too, was soon
able to return to her writing once she had acclimatized herself to
the new homeland.

Buber did not take long to master spoken Hebrew, and
though to begin with he wrote in German and then translated

his material with the help of a Hebraist, after a short time he was writing directly in Hebrew. The results were judged by some to be strange, as he tended to manipulate Hebrew in the same way that he treated German. But according to Maurice Friedman, it is not true, as some unfriendly critics have maintained, that his Hebrew was no good. 'Buber expressed himself very forcefully in that language.'[2]

Strange to say, the first full-scale book to emerge from the new life in the Middle East appeared first in the Netherlands in Dutch, in 1940.[3] It was published in Hebrew in 1942, in English as *The Prophetic Faith* in 1949, and in German at last as *Die Glaube der Propheten* in 1950. The explanation for the Dutch publication is that Buber was asked by Professor Gerardus van Leeuw of Groningen to take part in a planned collective study of the religions of the world. He was not at first eager, but when he heard that he would not only be the sole non-Dutchman contributing but also the only Jew, he decided to accept the challenge.

As is not altogether clear from the English title, the work sets out to be an exposition of the religion of the prophets of Israel. It aims to show how they served as mediators in a living dialogue between God and his people, promoting ideas and conceptions of the Deity which matched the people's needs and reminding them of the obligations demanded by the God they recognized. One divine form evolved from a preceding one, in turn influencing the shape of its successor, the God-idea changing, say, from a God of journeys, to a God of the fathers, to God the King, God the Warrior, God the Husband, God the Holy One to the Righteous One, to the Lord of the World, though not necessarily in that order. Every divine form entered history, played its part, and subsequently made way for a new form distinguished and proclaimed by another of the prophets.

Buber is, however, at pains to argue that different as all these notions have been, they have all at heart shared an identical divine nature. If God the Warrior, for example, may seem other than the Lord of the World, this is because the human partner of man-God relation changes. Israel's God himself remains one and the same, whatever temporary form he is seen to assume. He is always YHWH, whose Name, according to his own words to Moses, means *He is there*. He is present as whoever he is present. He is the Present One whose Presence takes whatever shape he himself chooses.

It is furthermore pointed out that if YHWH requires of himself that he should be present with his people, by the same token he looks for that to be his people's duty towards him. As YHWH does to them, so, within their capabilities, must they do to YHWH. The true worship of YHWH as taught by the prophets was to be evinced through Israel's presence with him.

The final section of the book, 'The God of the Sufferers', considers the prophets' condemnation of the Sanctuary, the suffering of the innocent and the mystery of the messianic redemption of the world. Here, Buber takes advantage of Jeremiah's famous Temple speech (Jer. 7) to advance his own ambivalence towards 'religion' as opposed to 'religiousness'. 'Amend your ways and your doings/ and I will let you dwell/ in this place./ Never assure yourselves with the words of the lie,/ the saying,/ This is HIS Temple, HIS Temple, HIS Temple'.* By this the prophet means that

> his God is not concerned with 'religion'. Other gods need
> a house, an altar, sacrifice, because without them they are
> not, because they consist only of what earthly beings give
> them. The living God and King of world-time (*Weltzeit*)
> needs none of this because he is. He desires no religion. He
> desires a human nation, human beings living with human
> beings, human makers of decisions to provide with their
> rights those who thirst for justice, strong to pity the weak
> (7:5 f), human beings associating with human beings.[4]

Jeremiah, one of the martyrs of the ancient world, who took upon himself the sufferings of his people and fulfilled for them their purification and *teshuvah*, witnessed and was the catalyst of one of the moments when a new divine form took over from the old. He saw YHWH leave his 'house' and move into the

* Buber actually renders the corresponding word *hekhal* as *Halle*, perhaps because of the similarity of sound, but the use of 'hall' in English would be misleading.

distant heavens, though always remaining close to the needy and distressed.

But the question always asked is, 'Why does he allow the innocent to suffer?' Or rather, as the Book of Job phrases it, 'Why does God "cause" the innocent to suffer?' Job sees him as a Being who permits Satan to wander the earth tempting men to sin. One of his comforters regards God as an avenger. But Job's own conclusion is that in 'hiding his Face' (13:24) from him, YHWH, *He is there*, is contradicting his own essential nature. When Job in his pain wishes to reason with God, to argue his own blamelessness, what he really wants, according to Buber, is God's own Presence with him once more. 'O that I knew where to find him,' he mourns (25:3). He fights against God's distance and silence, the God who rages against him and yet remains quiet. This absence of God's light is the real source of Job's despair. God's own view of himself, however, is that he is a just God who gives to each of his creatures all that it needs to be entirely itself. Man, Buber explains,

> is deliberately deficient in this presentation of heaven and earth, which shows him that a justice exists greater than his own, and that with this justice which aims to give each 'his due' he is called on merely to emulate divine justice which gives to each what he is.[5]

The lesson concerning the engima of suffering to be read in the Book of Job is associated in *The Prophetic Faith* with personal revelation, 'a particular revelation to an individual, revelation as a reply to the sufferer concerning the question of his suffering; God's limitation of himself to a Person who replies to a person.'[6] For Job's distress that God's 'lamp' no longer shines over him as in the time when the Almighty was 'yet with me', is eased at last, not so much because he comes to realize that he has been complaining from ignorance, as because he becomes aware that his spirit is once again in touch with God. He hears God's words with his 'ear' and can again see God's Presence with his 'eye'.

The book ends with a section called 'The Mystery', in which Buber looks at the teaching of Deutero-Isaiah (Isaiah 40–55) that

the redemption of Israel and that of the world are to be two
stages of the one great coming of the Kingdom of God. YHWH's
command is, 'Turn to me and be saved all the ends of the earth'
(45:22). But who is to be the agent of this universal *teshuvah*?
Who was, or who will be, the suffering Servant smitten, not for
the sins of Israel, which God himself will carry, but for the sins
of the 'nations'?

Buber suggests that the Servant will come from among the
prophets who mediate between heaven and earth. He will be
God's 'perfected one', his *meshullam*. Called on to direct the
'nations', he will establish God's Kingdom on earth. But as well
as this personal Servant, or rather identical with him, there will
be a corporate Servant, Israel. Israel is to be God's *meshullam*, his
stricken and afflicted one and his Messiah.

> Insofar as Israel's great suffering in the Diaspora is a
> suffering not merely endured but truly borne and per-
> formed, it is to be interpreted in the image of the Servant.
> Whoever in Israel does the suffering of Israel, is the
> Servant, and he is the Israel in whom YHWH is glorified.[7]

Buber possessed to a remarkable degree the ability to pass with
ease and speed from one subject to another totally different one,
and in the particularly fruitful nine years under review in the
present chapter, he moved from the Bible to Hasidism, to
philosophy, and back to the Bible, taking in on the way other
topics as varied as politics and education.

For the Sake of Heaven,[8] originally called in Hebrew *Gog
u-Magog*, was first serialized in the newspaper *Davar* in 1941 and
then appeared as a book in 1944. A collection of Hasidic stories
or 'sacred anecdotes' brought together to form not so much a
novel as a chronicle, it presents against a broad canvas of *hasidim*,
their wives, children, friends and opponents, a portrait of
nineteenth-century Hasidic life, with its magic tradition and its
anti-magic school, and with its great and saintly personalities
such as Rabbi Jacob Isaac of Lublin, nicknamed 'the Seer'
(d. 1815), and Rabbi Jacob Isaac of Pzhysha, known as 'the Jew' or
'the holy Jew' (d. 1813). The stories are mainly strung together

by means of dialogue, but retain enough action and colour for them to show how the Hasidic community, grouped around its leader the *zaddik*, converted Hasidic teachings and beliefs into the reality of 'lived life'.

With 'What is Man?'[9] Buber turns from Hasidism to philosophical anthropology and, with the assistance of thinkers ancient and modern, ranging from Aristotle to Max Scheler (d. 1928), considers man's changing concept of himself with the intention of presenting his own answer to the question he poses. Broadly speaking, his conclusions are as follows.

It is a characteristic of human history that periods during which people live happily at home in the world alternate with others in which they feel isolated and estranged from it. Another recurring feature is that it is in the times of alienation that they face up to the problem of what man is and respond to it in varying ways. It is when they feel alone, in a world become unfamiliar to them, that they reach out beyond it to something or someone who will mitigate their loneliness. But with each successive period of estrangement, God becomes more and more difficult to find and in the end cannot be discovered at all. He is then pronounced dead. At that point, the only solution remaining available is for man to reach out to himself. And this is what people do. Since it is no longer possible to communicate with a divine form of whatever kind, they are reduced to entering into intimate communion with themselves.

This approach is typified by the 'individualistic anthropology' of such thinkers as Hegel, Heidegger, Kierkegaard, which is concerned with relation within the self and with the self, for example between the mind and the instincts. But human beings can never understand themselves in this way. They only become comprehensible within the context of relation with other living beings.

At the same time, it is admittedly the solitary who above all can throw light on human nature. A way has therefore to be found in which isolation is overcome without damaging the particular ability to answer the question, what is man? The tension of solitude must be preserved, but in the context of a renewal of life with the world so that people can think from outside that situation.

The overcoming of isolation has been achieved in modern times in two ways: by applying the principles of individualism on the one hand, and those of collectivism on the other. Individualism lays stress on man in relation to himself. Collectivism ignores the individual and emphasizes 'society' instead. But neither of these treatments of the human situation—both of them essentially deriving from fear of the world and fear of life, the products of an existential exposure to solitariness of a magnitude probably never experienced before—has done anything to meet the human need. Individualism, with its glorification of separateness, has done no more to alleviate the misery of alienation than collectivism, with its submergence of the self in the group.

> The fundamental fact of human existence is neither the individual as such nor the totality as such ... What primarily distinguishes the human world is that something exists between being and being that appears nowhere else in nature.[10]

That something is speech. At this point Buber introduces the concept of the *between* already mentioned in *I and Thou* (see, e.g., the final paragraph) and due to reappear elsewhere, notably in *Paths in Utopia*. The *between*, he says, is where we should think of relation as taking place. It is not *in* the individual. It is not *in* the world. It is specifically and factually *between* two vis-à-vis. These three factors, the *I*, the *you* and the *between*, constitute both the situation and the conveyors of what takes place between two partners in dialogue.

Buber's own definition of man, or rather his suggestion concerning man, is therefore a dialogical one. We may come closer, he diffidently proposes,

> to the answer to the question, 'what is man?', when we learn to understand him as the being in whose dialogic, in whose reciprocally present two-ness, encounter of one with the other is realized and recognized.[11]

'What is Man?' was followed two years later by the much more substantial work *Moses*.[12] Buber's second biblical study to appear during the war years, his stated wish was to portray in it the prophet as a concrete personality and to relate his achievements unbiased by any religious tradition or academic school of thought. He rejected the theory that the biblical text of the Pentateuch is assembled from various 'sources'. He believed that each biblical episode rests on the adaptation of a tradition which has undergone through the ages a variety of treatments. The task demanded is to distinguish the early strata from later increments and to find a way back to the presumed tradition itself. Part of this work is not difficult because additions can be detected linguistically as well as by content; but for the rest one can only proceed by means of hypotheses.

Like *The Prophetic Faith* (with which it overlaps in places), *Moses* is an account of relation between man and God, and specifically with the God of Moses. The divine form it depicts is one who delivers, leads and fights for his people, the people's Prince and Law-Giver. He is a God

who appears, speaks and reveals. He is invisible and 'causes himself to be seen'—in whichever natural phenomenon or historical event he in each case wishes to be seen. He causes his word to be made known to the men he calls in such a way that it breaks out of them and they become a 'mouth' for God. He causes his spirit to seize whomsoever he has chosen, causes it to produce in him and through him the work of God.[13]

The biblical story, told in brief and succinct chapters, inevitably includes the story of the burning bush, where once again the Name is entered into and expounded, this time fully. The importance of this Name to a study of Buber is that it defines the nature of his concept of God, the Being referred to in *I and Thou* as the everlasting *You*. That *You* cannot of itself be a form of God. 'You' is nothing more than the personal pronoun with which a speaker who knows himself or herself as 'I' addresses another who also knows himself or herself as 'I'. It follows that for a proper understanding of the whole edifice of

Buber's life of dialogue, which builds up from the *I* and *you* of imperfect relation to the *I* and *You* of perfect relation, we have to have some idea of how he envisaged the *I* behind that everlasting *You*, the supreme *I* to whom man says *You*. This emerges from his exegesis of the words placed in God's mouth in Exodus 3.

The first step in this long postponed account must be to retell the familiar tale in an English as near as possible to the German, chiefly to help with presenting Buber's argument, but also to give a further example of the literary genre adopted by the translators, with its attention to rhythm in the interest of oral recitation, its reproduction of emphatic repetition, and the forcing of the vocabulary to oblige words to conform as closely as possible to the original. An explanation of the use of pronouns applied to God will emerge in due course.

One important point to recall is that in Hebrew the one imperfect tense covers present and future. Thus the word *ehyeh* means both 'I am there' and 'I will be there'.

> Mosheh was herdsman of the sheep of Yitro his father-in-law, priest of Midian.
> He led the sheep to the far side of the desert.
> He came to Horeb to the mountain of God.
> HIS messenger appeared to him in the blaze of a fire from the midst of a thornbush.
> He looked;
> behold the thornbush burns in the fire yet the thornbush is unconsumed.
> Mosheh said,
> I will go over
> and see this great sight,
> why the thornbush is unconsumed.
> But when HE saw that he went over to see,
> God called him from the midst of the thornbush.
> He said,
> Mosheh! Mosheh!
> And he said,
> Here I am!
> He said,

Pull off your shoes from your feet,
for the place on which you stand is sanctifying ground.
And said,
I am your father's God,
the God of Abraham,
the God of Yitzhak,
the God of Ya'acob.
Mosheh hid his face,
for he was afraid to look at God.
But HE said,
I have seen, seen, the oppression of my people who are in
       Egypt.
I have heard their cry before their taskmasters.
Indeed, I have known their sufferings.
I have come down
to deliver them from the hand of Egypt,
to bring them up from out of that land
to a land good and spacious,
a land flowing with milk and honey,
the place of the Canaanites and the Hittites,
the Amorites and the Perizzites,
the Hivites and the Jebusites.
Now,
behold the cry of the sons of Israel has come to me.
And I have seen also the torment with which the
       Egyptians torment them.
Now go;
I send you to Pharaoh.
Lead my people, the sons of Israel, out of Egypt!
Mosheh said to God,
Who am I,
that I should go to Pharaoh,
that I should lead the sons of Israel out of Egypt?
But he said,
Surely, *I will be there* with you.
And this is the sign for you that I myself have sent you:
when you have led the people out of Egypt,
you shall on this mountain serve God. (Ex. 3:1–12)

With this, the first part of the dialogue comes to an end. When Moses demurs at the task laid on him, God says, 'Surely, *ehyeh* with you.' Buber translates the term *ehyeh*, the first person singular imperfect of the verb *hayah* or *hawah*, not as 'I am' or 'I will be' in the static abstract sense, of which he claims the Bible has as yet no notion, but as a dynamic and existential 'I am/I will become', 'I am/I will be there'. Accordingly, he sees in '*I will be there with you*' not simply an assurance of the divine Presence with Moses, but a clue also to the significance of the name *Yahweh*, which is taken to be the third person singular imperfect of the same verb, meaning 'He is/he will be there'.

The story continues:

Mosheh said to God,
I come then to the sons of Israel,
I say to them, The God of your fathers sends me to you.
They will say to me, What is there about his Name?
What shall I say to them? (3:13).

Here, the peculiarity of the Buber/Rosenzweig version is that instead of asking, 'What is his name?', Moses foresees being asked the *meaning* of God's Name. In addition to a fully developed philological argument for such a rendering, Buber suggests that it is hardly likely that the Israelites would have had to ask Moses for the name of their God.

Another consideration is that the environment of that time was one of magic and the occult. It was thought that to know a person's 'true' name was to have him in one's power. The Israelites would have imagined that, once in possession of the secret of the divine Name, they would be able to bend their Deity to their wishes and desires. But according to the novel Buber/Rosenzweig rendering, God said to Moses in answer to his question simply:

'*I will be there such as I will be there*' (3:14).

Not 'I am that I am' as the Revised Standard Version gives it, that is to say, but '*I am (I will be) there such as I am (I will be) there*'. It is this sentence that Buber distinguishes as the revelation of revelations, the climax of the whole story of the burning bush. No theological pronouncement would have been appreciated by the Israelites in their distress, nor any information about God's immutability or eternity. It is even, Buber says, impossible to justify 'I am that I am' on the grounds of language, for if the first *ehyeh* means 'I will be there', so must every succeeding *ehyeh*. God will be there, he tells Moses, not in any form that the people anticipate or choose, but as he himself desires and wills. And once more *ehyeh* is repeated:

And he said:
Thus shall you say to the sons of Israel,
I am there sends me to you   (3:14).

God describes himself by what he does, by what it is in his nature to do.

And God said further to Mosheh:
HE,
the God of your fathers,
the God of Abraham, the God of Yitzhak, the God of
    Yaacob,
sends me to you.
This is my Name in world-time,
my remembrance for generation after generation   (13:15).

The innovation at this point is of course the substitution of HE for YHWH. Buber and Rosenzweig had to find a way of transferring their reading of YHWH from one language to another without losing any of the undertones of presence implicit in the original. The logical step would seem to opt for HE IS THERE, paraphrases such as 'the LORD' being unacceptable because they replace fact with fiction: YHWH is a name, not a title. It was therefore decided to *re*-interpret the interpretation *He is there* in such a way that the appearance of YHWH in the text is signalled by the appropriate pronoun only. This strange device was mainly due to Franz Rosenzweig. When YHWH speaks, the Name is given as I and MY; when he is spoken to, as YOU and YOUR; and when he is spoken about, as HE, HIM and HIS. 'I am YHWH' (Ex. 6:3) thus becomes, 'It is *I*'; and 'On the day that YHWH God created . . .' becomes, as we have seen, 'On the day that HE, God, created . . .'

The next subject discussed in *Moses* is the first Passover, which Buber regarded as a sacramental meal, a 'holy and ancient shepherd's meal' renewed for the sake of uniting God with his people whom Moses was about to lead into freedom. The 'Passover of YHWH', celebrated in the family with shoes on the feet and a stave in the hand in readiness for a journey, was eventually to be transformed into a great yearly feast held in the Temple of Jerusalem.

To these two renewals—a renewed understanding of God's Name and a renewed sacramental meal—Buber adds a renewal of the Sabbath. The Sabbath was already ancient by the time of the Ten Commandments, but Moses renewed it to create 'a holy order of time'. Like other spiritual leaders, the prophet was not so much concerned to found a religion as to

> order a human world under a divine truth, to unite the ways of earth with those of heaven; and it is an essential part of this that time, which in itself is articulated only through cosmic rhythms, through the sun's changes and the phases of the moon, should become consolidated in a supreme holiness, one extending even beyond the cosmos. Thus Moses institutes the Sabbath, and with it the week flowing into the Sabbath, as the divine measure regulating the life of human beings. But the God whose measure it is, is precisely he who accepts man, is with him, frees him and helps him to salvation. Hence the Sabbath week cannot be only an 'absolute metre of time'; it is also of necessity an ever-returning way to the peace of God.[14]

Concerning the Commandments, Buber believed it must have been primarily Moses who 'raised imageless worship to a principle, or rather the imageless existence (*Dasein*) of the Invisible who permits himself to be seen'.[15]

Another problem confronted in this book is why the Commandments given are precisely these ten and not others. Buber's view is that they are not some kind of catechism. The soul of the Decalogue is its use of 'you'. The words are directed by the 'I' of God to the 'you' of whoever listens, but also to the 'you' of the community of which the individual is part; and for a community to subsist, not only must its life, marriage, property and social honour be preserved, they must also be protected against threatening attitudes such as covetousness, lust and envy.

Meditation on the Ark of YHWH and on the Tent of Encounter allows for a further expatiation on the divine Presence, and also on the prophetic spirit in its manifestations of ecstasy and prediction. With which of these elements was Moses associated? According to Buber, with neither. Moses was special. The passage is cited from Numbers 11:24 in which, because the people have complained about their inadequate food, Moses summons the elders to the Tent of Encounter. There, YHWH 'came down in a cloud' and spoke to him, and afterwards distributed some of the spirit that rested on him among the seventy elders and they too prophesied. Later, Miriam and Aaron criticized Moses and argued that in the incident of the Tent he was not the only one to prophesy. YHWH had spoken through them too. At this, God was angry. The rest, he said, had heard him in a dream and seen him in a vision. But not so his servant Moses.

> In all my house he is trusty,
> mouth to mouth I speak to him,
> clearly and not in riddles
> he perceives my form.
> Therefore do not dare to speak against my servant, against
>   Mosheh!
> HIS anger flamed up and he went.

These words, Buber thought, conceal some dim recollection

> of a man who recognized his God, visually in his natural appearances, the God who is each time there such as he is there, and experienced his word as breathed into his inmost self. This is classically Israelite, and yet in its purity and power, unique.[16]

Moses finishes with the prophet's own end. He dies 'by the mouth of YHWH' and as Buber remarks, from the fact that the text mentions that 'he' buried Moses, it was obviously thought

that YHWH himself had dug his servant's final resting-place.
Hence 'no man knows his grave until this day', (Deut. 34).

From the very outset of his life in Palestine, Buber took his
stand in defence of Arab rights, continuing the pleas he had
made in earlier years. By 1938 he was writing:

> It is no wonder that the powers of darkness succeed, that
> young people struck by blindness place themselves in their
> service, and that people from among the public enthuse
> over their acts of violence. The situation has become so
> depressing that one can understand that more and more
> voices are raised among the people saying, 'If we cannot
> protect ourselves from the wolves, it is better that we too
> become wolves.' They forget that we have begun this
> work in this land in order to become whole *human beings*
> once more.[17]

At the same time, Buber could never even contemplate
relinquishing the Jewish claim to the land. The unity of the
people and Israel he regarded as fundamental to Jewish existence. He observes in *On Zion: the History of an Idea*:[18]

> The God of history and the God of nature cannot be
> separated and the land is a token of their unity. The God
> who brought Israel into this land, it is even he whose eyes
> are always upon it, 'from the beginning of the year even
> unto the end of the year' (Deut. 11:12)... that unique
> historical act in which God led the people with whom he
> had made the covenant into the promised land.

But the fact of the matter was that whereas when he was in
Germany Buber had struggled valiantly to animate and propagate a sense of Jewish solidarity and inspire Zionist enthusiasm,
once in Palestine he found he had to adopt a somewhat different
approach. Here, the governing need was for a cooling down an
overheated nationalism bordering on a fanaticism which sporad-
ically lost sight of all concern for ordinary humanity. In
resistance to this he formed in 1942, with Judah Magnes,
President of the Hebrew University, Ernst Simon and

Chaim Kalvarisky, Henrietta Szold, Zionist, philanthropist and life-long friend of Magnes, Gavriel Stern and Mosheh Smilansky, a Hebrew writer, a group calling itself Ichud, unity. With them, he lent his weight in urgently pressing for the co-operation of Jews and Arabs and for the development of a bi-national state. The group's aim was to win sympathy from Arab and Jewish intellectuals and to further mutual understanding and compromise.

Ichud was not a new development on the Zionist front but followed in the footsteps of B'rit Shalom, Covenant of Peace, which was created in 1925 and lasted till the mid-thirties, when it gave way under attacks from other Zionist parties. Its aim, too, had been to encourage Arab-Jewish relations and to work for a bi-national state. Among its charter members were Hugo Bergman and Hans Kohn. Gershom Scholem joined its ranks later, as did also Ernst Simon. In fact, B'rit Shalom was limited to a small intellectual circle, but various political figures, such as David Ben-Gurion, often took part in its proceedings.

Ichud appeared before an Anglo-American convention called by Ernest Bevin in 1946 to debate a memorandum drawn up by the group to the effect that Palestine should never become either a Jewish or an Arab state. It should be the homeland of both peoples, each having full autonomy, in which the reborn Jewish people would live in 'true community' with the Arabs and promote the prosperity of the land for both their sakes. Moreover, an internationally guaranteed agreement would ensure the preservation of peace between the two.

All this was in vain. In November 1947, the United Nations recommended partition. The Jews were to be allotted eastern Galilee, the northern Jordan valley, the valleys of Beth Shean and Jezreel, the coastal strip from a point south of Acre to a point south of Rehovot, together with the Negev, including Eilat on the Red Sea. Jerusalem was to be internationalized. (Ichud itself ceased temporarily on the outbreak of war in Palestine in 1948 and the death of Magnes, was revived in the 1950s, and finally was dissolved in 1964.)

It is some indication of the feeling aroused among Jews by the stand taken by Ichud that a letter, written by Buber and published in the Hebrew daily *Ha'aretz*, was rejected by the editor of the *Palestine Post* on the grounds that 'it is a Quisling-ism and a stab in the back of the Jewish cause'.[19]

In July 1947, Buber had written to Magnes. His message, he said, was a personal one but he wished his friends to read it. It came from the depths of his soul and should sink into the depths of their souls also. Some years ago, he told Magnes,

> when I was fighting for a Jewish-Arab treaty at the Zionist Congress, I had an experience that shocked me and was to determine my future life. I had outlined a resolution emphasizing the community of interests of the two nations and presenting a way of collaboration be-tween them—the only way that can lead to the salvation of the land and its two peoples. Before the resolution was presented to the Congress for ratification it came before an editorial committee which was to establish its final form. Naturally, I was a member of this committee. Then something happened that is quite usual and ordinary for a professional politician, but so shocked me that until this day I have not managed to recover from it. In the editorial committee, which for the most part consisted of old friends of mine, first one small amendment was recommended, and then another small amendment, and yet another amendment ... Each one individually had no apparent significance and the reason for them all was that the resolution should be acceptably formulated for the Congress. Repeatedly, I heard the words, 'Do you just want to make a demonstration, or do you wish Congress to endorse the basis of Jewish–Arab collaboration and fight for it? If the latter, you must agree to the small amendments.' Naturally, it was not a case of demon-strating; I wanted a change of attitude of the Zionist movement towards the Arab problem. I therefore struggled for my own proposed text, but gave in more and more, and waived it when the affair depended on it. When the editorial committe had finished its work and brought a fair copy of the agreed text to me in the hotel, I

saw a series of fine and convincing sentences, but the marrow and blood of my original demand were no longer in them. I accepted the business and gave my consent for the resolution to be brought before the Congress. I contented myself, in a personal explanation prior to the reading of the resolution and the vote, with emphasizing the *fundamental* turn which I had in view with my motion. But I felt that my role as 'politician', i.e. as someone who takes part in the political activity of a group, was finished. I had taken up a cause and had had to bring it to an end. I could not take up a new cause in which I would again be placed before the choice between truth and realization. From then on, I had to renounce 'resolutions' and be satisfied with 'personal talks'.

Many years thus passed until I came to Eretz Israel and saw how you, my friend, were trying to promote the same radical struggle for Jewish–Arab collaboration which eventually assumed the form of our Ichud. The fact that you did so, and the way you did it, have been a great gift of life to me: you have made it possible for me to work politically once more within the context, and in the name of, a political group without sacrificing truth. You understand my meaning. I am not concerned for the purity and salvation of my soul; if ever it should be the case—which in the nature of things is impossible—that I had to choose between the saving of my soul and the salvation of my people, I know I would not hesitate. It is a question of not violating the truth, since I have come to know that truth is the seal of God (BT *Shabbath* 55a), while we are the wax in which this seal seeks to be stamped. The older I grow, the clearer this becomes, and I feel that in this we are brothers. To you, too, it becomes clearer every day. But from where we stand, there has for a long time been no longer any choice. There is no opposition between the truth of God and the salvation of Israel.[20]

7

THE FINAL DECADES

The foundation of the State of Israel was declared in 1948. Horrors abounded on all sides and the mass exodus of the Arabs, encouraged by the neighbouring States, was further prompted by atrocity stories. In effect, the seeds were sown of the political situation in the Middle East as we now know it. During this time of great strain, however, Buber continued to retain the Arabs' respect.

On his seventieth birthday on 8 February, Judah Magnes published his good wishes in a special edition of *Ba'ayot*. The letter is very revealing, in regard to both the conditions then prevailing in Israel and Buber's own attitude to them. Magnes begins by recalling his first sight of Buber attending a lecture given by Georg Simmel in Berlin in the academic year 1900–1, and then goes on:

> Of all the greatness that you have produced in this half century from the treasures of your profound and noble spirit, especially since you came to the Land, people will speak among the circles of the wise and clever not only now but in the days to come. Today, I cannot restrain myself, but must devote my words to the tragic events which are taking place during these days as you enter the 'club' of the hoary seventies.
>
> The tragedy of these days is not that after dancing and jubilation over the UNO decision [of 29 November 1947, partitioning Palestine and internationalizing Jerusalem] confusion and anxiety now reign, or the loss of dear and irrevocable human life, or the fighting and more fighting, the end of which cannot be foreseen. The tragedy is that today, as in the days of the prophet Micah (3:9–10), the

'heads of the house of Jacob and the lords of the house of Israel build Zion with blood'—though with changes of nuance and definition corresponding to the circumstances of the time.

You thought and believed that Zion could be built not with blood and fire but with untiring creative work, and by means of mutual understanding with our neighbours. You know quite well that in the history of humanity States have almost always been established only with blood and injustice. But you counted too much on miracles, for at least since the days of Rabbi Yohanan ben Zakkai until our own time, religious tradition, the tradition of Judaism, has considered the shedding of blood as the national arch-sin. The terrible sufferings which our people had to suffer were so unbearable that they robbed us of the ability to be patient. We were unable to be satisfied for a further length of time with daily creative work and we became subject to the *fata morgana* of the State, as though it were a shield which could protect us against the enmity of the nations.

You see now the wreckage of almost everything that was dear to you. In Eretz Israel, out of the house of Israel a nation has come into being that is like all other nations; and it has no faith in election, or in the religion and ethical mission of the people of Israel. You see the younger generation and their teachers, priests and prophets going before them, as they create their gods in their own likeness, and leaping and dancing proclaim the molten calf which they themselves have made. 'This is your God, O Israel.' You see with how much satisfaction the Holy Land is dismembered and the horse-trading over its parts. You see how all your efforts to instil into the nation a spirit of mutual understanding with its neighbours have come to nothing. You the man of spirit *par excellence* must suffer spiritual torment when it becomes clear to you that in the people of Israel, your own people, spirit has no actual effect, but only the fist and violence. You unite in yourself two qualities which viewed superficially contradict one another . . .

Do you look into the future with extreme pessimism? God grant that there will be no new destruction. It is in any case my wish for you today that you do not allow your courage to sink; that it may be given to you to continue the struggle with true reality as ever; that you may be granted long life so that you may see HIS return to Zion in truth and mercy.[1]

As far as publishing was concerned, 1947 had seen the appearance in their definitive form, and in English, of Buber's *Tales of the Hasidim*. These two volumes, covering the early and later masters, record in the form of anecdotes teachings of the various *zaddikim* and of the founder of Hasidism himself, the Ba'al Shem Tov. Of great charm and appeal, these have probably been as influential, if not more so, than Buber's more austere and demanding *I and Thou*.

This was also the year in which Buber made his first return to Europe, visiting, as he told the publisher Salman Schocken in a letter in July, six countries, which included France (the Sorbonne) and London (the London School of Economics, whose director at that time was Harold Laski), and giving in all sixty lectures. Afterwards he and Paula spent several weeks in Switzerland. Buber was especially struck by his reception in the Netherlands and England, though the French reaction had been more intellectual he thought. But all in all he had been agreeably surprised by the spiritual liveliness met with in the West.

Another event of 1947 was the publication in Hebrew of the book which became known in English, in 1949, as *Paths in Utopia*. Once again breaking new ground, it has been greatly admired even by readers unable to get very far with Buber's other writings. In it, Buber, who regarded himself as a Utopian Socialist, meditates on the topic of political idealism and follows the various experiments in Utopian Socialism with a view to proposing as examples of 'signal non-failure'[2] the village communes of Israel.

Utopianism Buber describes as 'an image of what should be, of what the image-maker desires shall be':[3] in other words, a fantasy constructed around a wish. It is a desire for rightness which, if experienced philosophically, appears as an image of perfect *space*, and if experienced as revelation, is projected as an image of perfect *time* in the form of a messianic eschatology. In the first instance, it is by nature limited to human society, though it sometimes demands the transformation of the individual. In the second, it extends by nature beyond the confines of human life. Both kinds of Utopianism can be realized only in community.

Another even more important difference is that whereas Utopianism as an image of perfect space is entirely dependent on the human will, as an image of perfect time the decisive action comes mainly from above, with nevertheless, in its elementary prophetic stage, a share allotted to man also.

The Utopianism associated with revelation has with the passage of time gradually lost its impact. It has become increasingly difficult to believe in action from above which will save the world. By contrast, technology and the social inconsistencies of the present age have had such a profound effect on Utopianism as a notion of perfect space that even the will on which the creation of a new social order is seen to depend is now understood technically. In addition, the forces of the displaced messianism have now been turned to the service of this Utopian social system and the proclamation and summons which were formerly the prerogative of religion are now heard issuing from Socialism and Communism.

As the fathers of Utopian Socialism, Buber recognizes Saint-Simon (d. 1825), Fourier (d. 1837) and Owen (d. 1858), and subsequently Proudhon (d. 1865) and Kropotkin (d. 1921). Following an outline of the theories of these men, he goes on to discuss those of his friend Gustav Landauer, an anarchist rather than a Socialist.

Landauer's Utopian vision was of a society in which individuals would not need to be taught how to live with one another but would learn by personal example. Thus, if Socialism is a form of secular messianism, with Marxists as its apocalyptics foretelling history and its catastrophes, Landauer and his predecessors were its prophets calling for *teshuvah*. He was convinced that true religion would be the *outcome* of a regenerated society rather than its cause. His 'communities of love' were to be religion realized.

Buber's own reflections on a community coincided with Landauer's. To be authentic, a community had to be one of need, and for that reason a community of spirit. It had to be one of endeavour and work, and for that reason a community of salvation.

After looking into some of the brave yet failed Utopian ventures, Buber moves on in the book to those of Marx, Engels and Lenin. Utopian Socialism, he explains, looks for the replacement of the State by society to the highest degree. Karl Marx came close to this end, but ultimately found it an impossible task, as he also found it impossible to provide an answer to the problem of the interrelation of smaller social units in the reconstruction of society as a whole. Of the deformation that ensued, Buber writes:

> It [Marxism] gathered the proletariat around it with great powers of recruitment and organization. It acted with great pugnacity in attack and defence in the political and economic field. But that for which in the last resort it had recruited and organized and fought—the development of a new social form—was neither the true object of its awareness nor the true goal of its action ... It did not look to the pre-forms of a new society already existing. It did not bother itself seriously with promoting, influencing, leading, co-ordinating and federating newly developed experiments or those in the process of formation. It did not itself, with consistent work, call into being the cells and associations of cells of living community. With its great powers, it did not lend its hand to re-shaping the new human social existence which was to be liberated by the revolution.[4]

With Marx and Lenin, it was not the idea of an organic reconstruction of a new greater society out of smaller societies linked by ties of a common life and work that provided the context for positive action. It was rather that the tendency towards decentralization was supplanted by a centralization of politics. Marx required that the political principle should be superseded by the social, but he continued to steer in a political direction.

With a final chapter, entitled 'An experiment that did not fail', Buber concludes that the one comprehensive attempt to create a new society to have met with some success is the village commune and the collectivist working community in Israel: the *kvutzah* and the *kibbutz*. But even they have not always developed smoothly in three respects: 1) in the growth of a sense of community in the smaller group; 2) in the growth of federal sense between one smaller group and another; and 3) in the growth of the federated groups into a changed greater society. Compared with Soviet Russia, they have nevertheless not failed, and one reason for this, Buber suggests, is that the *kvutzah* owes its existence to circumstances and not to theory. Another is that ideals have gone hand in hand with motives and have consequently remained flexible. A third, even more weighty reason than the others is that external crisis aroused a great inner response which threw up an élite, the *haluzim*, or pioneers. The Israeli communes are not failures, Buber repeats, but neither are they successes. Yet until Russia itself

experiences an essential inner change—and we cannot yet guess when and how this will happen—we must designate by the mighty name of 'Moscow' one of the two poles of Socialism between which we have to choose. The other pole, despite everything, I would venture to name 'Jerusalem'.[5]

Buber's eighth decade, although his popularity among his fellow-countrymen was not excessive, was in many ways the richest and busiest of his life. He founded in 1949, and for four years directed, a training college for teachers in adult education. He resumed his work on the German translation of the Bible, published two very important books, *Two Types of Faith* and *Eclipse of God*, and in 1951 was awarded the Hanseatic Goethe Prize, which he accepted, thereby attracting to himself a good deal of obloquy at home. The money was donated by him to *Ner* (light), the monthly journal of Ichud.

Buber had by then relinquished his university post and was free to travel extensively. In December 1951 he visited the United States for the first time and established contacts with American Jewry. *I and Thou* had not been translated until 1937, but after the war many more of his works appeared in English. It was a taxing journey—he was by now seventy-three years old—which took him all over the continent, from the Jewish Theological Seminary in New York, to the University of Judaism in Los Angeles and the College of Jewish Studies in Chicago, and he spoke in addition at the universities of Yale, Chicago, Brandeis, Cornell, Stanford, North Carolina and Princeton, and at the New York School for Social Research. Maurice Friedman wrote to him after his departure from the United States to say that he and his wife had frequently been unhappy to see how hard he had had to work and how tired he had often been.[6] The enterprise was rounded off with a farewell celebration in a packed Carnegie Hall, at which the Protestant theologian Reinhold Niebuhr spoke, as well as Mordechai Kaplan, the founder of the Reconstructionist movement in Judaism, and of course Buber himself.

Another visit to Europe followed in 1953–4, when he lectured and held discussions in Switzerland and Holland and spent some time in Tübingen in Germany. More importantly, he returned to Frankfurt to receive the Peace Prize of the German Book Trade. As before, when he was given the Goethe Prize, his acceptance excited considerable criticism, especially on the part of Holocaust survivors. He was attacked in the Israeli papers and in the English and American Jewish press for what appeared to be his leniency towards the Germans. But it is noteworthy that the speech he delivered on that day appears in *Nachlese*, which he expressly describes as a collection of what he felt to be most worthwhile among his writings.

Ten years ago, he told the crowd assembled for the prize-giving ceremony, several thousand Germans murdered millions of Jews with a ferocity unequalled in history. Such a huge distance separated these people from true humanity that he could not even hate them. And who was he to 'forgive'? There were also Germans who knew what was going on in Auschwitz and Treblinka but did nothing about it. These he could not condemn. Familiar with human weakness, he could not sit in judgement on people unable to embrace martyrdom. Similarly, in the case of those who were ignorant of the facts but did nothing to find out what lay behind rumours, he was well aware of the human anxiety not to search for something which might turn out to be unbearable. However, there were some who refused to obey the orders of their superiors and suffered death themselves. They, Buber said, were quite near to him in that special intimacy that binds us to the dead, and to them alone, and there was reverence and love for those Germans in his heart.

The remainder of the address, after a brief mention of the young who had nothing to do with their country's crime and whose spirit, he felt sure, had been made the more alert by the recollection of those years, is concerned with the crisis of modern man, which he ascribes above all to an incapacity to communicate. Nation cannot speak to nation. Why should this be? Because we have lost confidence in each other and in life. We are uncertain whether life has any meaning. Meanwhile, in the background lurks *homo contrahumanus*—Satan, the Hinderer—waiting to take advantage of *homo humanus* locked in his international misunderstandings. Let us not permit this Satanic power ever again to sweep through the world, Buber pleaded. Let us redeem speech from the ban placed on it. Let us have confidence despite everything.

Still another tour in 1956 took Buber to London, to the Sorbonne again, and to the Free University of Berlin, where he spoke on the meaning of Hasidism for western man. The following year, 1957, he travelled once more to the United States, where he was by this time famous. Michigan University, for example, held a Buber week which included sessions given by himself and discussions of his work by others. He also lectured at the School of Psychiatry in Washington on 'Elements of the Interhuman', 'Distance and Relation' and 'Guilt and Guilt Feelings', papers which, together with three other essays and a dialogue between Buber and the psychologist Carl Rogers, recorded by Maurice Friedman at The Midwest Conference at

Michigan, make up the book *The Knowledge of Man*, published in 1965.

The last journey that Buber made to the United States was in 1958, when he was eighty. On the way back to Israel he spoke in Cologne at the Volkshochschule, but on 2 August in Venice, where he and Paula were to take a ship to Israel, she was suddenly struck down by a thrombosis and was taken to hospital. Their daughter Eva stayed with her, and Buber himself moved into a nearby hotel, hoping that Paula would recover and they could leave at the end of the month. However, inflammation of the lungs set in and she died on 11 August. 'We have buried her,' Buber wrote to Friedman, 'I and my children, in the old cemetery of the Jewish community here on the Lido, full of old trees.'[7] Buber was unwell for some months following this great loss and later went to Switzerland and Germany to convalesce. But he was no longer capable of the same tremendous output of energy as before.

Two Types of Faith, first published in 1950,[8] carries a Foreword paying tribute to Rudolf Bultmann for 'fundamental instruction in New Testament exegesis', to Albert Schweitzer 'for what he gave me to know directly through his person and his life', and to the authority on comparative religion Rudolf Otto, for his 'profound understanding of the divine majesty in the Hebrew Bible' and 'the noble frankness with which he opened to me his believing heart in peripatetic conversations'. He also gives thanks to the spirit of Leonhard Ragaz, professor of theology at Zürich, who foresaw

> a future [of] as yet unimaginable understanding between the kernel of the community of Israel and a genuine community of Jesus, which would arise, neither on a Jewish nor on a Christian foundation, but on the message common to both Jesus and the prophets concerning man's *teshuvah* and the Kingdom of God.[9]

That these sentiments of Ragaz were also Buber's own is apparent from the underlying tenor of the work, which argues that the faith of Jesus was not that of Christianity but of Judaism, but that the faith of Christianity, with its emphasis on the individual, nevertheless possesses virtues which Judaism needs in order to remain a true and living religion.

Belief, so the reasoning goes, whatever the subject of faith may be, is either belief that something is true or belief in someone. It is either *pistis* (Greek) or *emunah* (Hebrew). *Pistis*, a characteristic of early Christianity, involves above all an act of the mind; Thomas, when he saw the risen Jesus, exclaimed 'My Lord and my God', was the first to testify to it.[10] *Emunah*, typical of Judaism, is an acceptance of divine sovereignty demonstrated by means of obedience to God's will in everyday life. Thus the position of a religious person professing *pistis* is that of someone converted to his faith, who consequently helps to generate a community of other converted individuals. The position by contrast of one professing *emunah* is that of someone who, so to speak, finds himself in a community whose bond with God includes him also.

Buber is careful to point out that such statements are only generalizations and are intended merely to mean that *pistis* and *emunah* are typified by Judaism and Christianity.

One point he is not shy of making in *Two Types of Faith* is the contrast between the teaching of Paul and that of Jesus. Whereas by preaching *teshuvah*, a return to a spirit of trust, obedience and love, Jesus exemplified his own *emunah* and asked it of his disciples, Paul never speaks of the love of God. Indeed, in the translation of Jesus' teaching for the Greek world, *teshuvah* loses its comprehensiveness and instead of signifying a turning back to God of the whole self, comes through the Greek word *metanoia* to mean only a change of 'mind'. Paul furthermore never repeats Jesus' insistence on immediacy of relation beween man and God. For Paul, it is as though a wall had been erected around the Godhead since Jesus taught 'Ask and you shall receive, knock and it shall be opened to you.' To whomsoever finds that door, God, who has redeemed the world shows his grace. But whosoever remains far from it is given up to Satan and his angels.

Again, in the Sermon on the Mount, Jesus speaks like the Pharisees as though it is possible, both literally and in accordance with its inward purpose, to fulfil the Law. Paul contests this, provoking Buber to assert that he either did not realize that he was contradicting Jesus, or, which is more likely, his attitude was in some way connected with his decision or necessity not to know Christ any longer 'after the flesh'. This would mean acknowledging that what Jesus preached was appropriate to the time in which he lived but was not needed after his death and resurrection.

Paul's thesis is that the God of Israel gave his people a Law on which they would certainly come to grief, with the deliberate intention, in his planned salvation, of making them obdurate 'until the full count of the Gentiles has entered in' (Rom. 11:25). 'When I contemplate this God,' Buber notes with distaste,

> 'I do not recognize the God of Jesus, nor if I contemplate this world do I see it as his. For Jesus, who was concerned with individual human souls and with each individual human soul, Israel was not a generality ... Neither was it merely the totality of Jews living in his time and in relation to his message. All the souls who had lived between Moses and himself were *in concreto* part of it. In his view, *teshuvah* was assured for every one of them if they had gone astray, and each one making his *teshuvah* was the lost son returning home. His God was ever the same, who in all generations, though he might at times harden himself and at times even give a statute that was not good, answered the soul representing Israel with, "I have forgiven in accordance with your words" (Num. 14:20). In Paul's image of God, this characteristic is replaced by another where the generations of souls between Moses and Jesus are concerned. I do not dare to name it.'[11]

As for Jesus 'the son of God', or as he puts it, 'the God Jesus', this deification is seen by Buber not as a caprice but a compulsion, a process, which is how all new forms of the Godhead come into being, ever and always. At the same time, no such divine form as this has happened in Israel before. Where Israel in terms of religious history means relation between man and a God who allows himself to be seen in events and natural phenomena while remaining invisible, Christianity has presented one with a human face, that of a 'suffering God' a 'great saviour God'. 'The God of Christians is at once imageless and imaged, imageless in the religious idea, imaged in the lived present. The image conceals the Imageless One.'[12]

The various periods of Christian history can be classified according to how much or how little Paulinism predominates, Buber maintains. The present age is particularly Pauline.

> A Paulinism of the unredeemed exists, one therefore from which the stronghold of grace is eliminated. Here, the world is experienced as Paul experienced it, as in the hands of ineluctable powers, and only the manifest redeeming will from above, only Christ, is missing. The Christian Paulinism of our time is the fruit of the same fundamental view, though it weakens or removes the aspect of the demonization of the government of the sphere of expiation whence the call goes up clearly and vigorously for the establishment of a Christian way of life, but where the unredeemed Christian soul *de facto* confronts an unredeemed human world in noble powerlessness.[13]

Pistis and *emunah* are both in crisis now. *Emunah* lacks any psychological foundation in the State of Israel, and any vital basis in a religion isolated from the national life. The essential spontaneity of personal religion runs the risk of eventual impoverishment in an age of the eclipse of God such as our own, and may be succeeded by elements of *pistis* partly rational and partly mystical by nature. On the other hand, the divorce of personal holiness from national holiness presents a danger to *pistis*. With its origin in the individual and outside the national experience, it is a commitment *whereby* he or she sets him or herself apart from the nation. With the idea of a holy nation displaced by a church that is 'a people of God', the existence of a Christian is divided into a personal life and life as a participant in that of the nation. All will be well as long as the personal is able to hold its own against the public sphere, but there is a danger in the disparity between the holiness of the person and the accepted unholiness of the community, a disparity necessarily transferred to the 'inner dialectic of the human soul'.

To end his book, Buber returns to the tone sounded at the beginning. *Pistis* and *emunah* need one another. Christianity and Judaism are essentially different and will remain so until mankind is gathered in from the 'exiles of the religions' into the Kingdom of God. But an Israel striving for the renewal of its faith through the rebirth of the holy person, and a Christianity striving for the renewal of its faith through the rebirth of the holy nation, may have help as yet unsuspected to offer one another and something as yet unsaid to say to one another.

Buber's last work of substance was *Eclipse of God: Studies in the Relation between Religion and Philosophy*, which was published in 1953. A collection of lectures delivered originally in various American universities, their general theme is that perceptible in so many of his later writings, namely that God is not dead, as Nietzsche announced. It is just that the Face of man's everlasting Vis-à-Vis has become temporarily obscured.

Each historical age is distinguished by the prevailing relationship between religion and reality. Periods in which the subject of belief possesses an existence of its own, when people feel themselves in real relation with it, even though they may have a most hazy idea of what it is that they believe in, alternate with other times when the reality believed in becomes merely an *idea* of that reality, an idea that people 'have' and can manipulate. Such is the age in which we live. Our unreality manifests itself insofar as we 'think' religion instead of 'doing' it. It has become the property of the mind rather than of the whole person.

Moreover, in failing to recognize present existence as the medium through which we may hear and do the requirements of God, we have admitted an element of magic into religion, or what passes as religion today. We find it in order to ask, without bothering to listen for what is demanded in return. We try to put pressure on a God who can be used. The magical tendency, evident in the attempts of *soi-disant* theosophists and even theologians to unveil the Mystery and make it comprehensible, comes from worshipping the Supreme Being ritually without truly communing with him.

For at the heart of the contemporary unreality of religion is unreality of prayer. Once prayer is infected with the self-consciousness typical of religion today, immediacy between man and God breaks down. Prayer in its precise sense is a plea to God for his Presence to be made known. The one prerequisite for that Presence is therefore unreserved spontaneity and readiness for that Presence on the part of the whole man. No one who is not himself present can become aware of presence.

Philosophy's contribution to this dilemma is that from having treated God as an object it now ignores him altogether. As the unreality of the prevailing divine forms becomes reflected in the unreality of the religions confessing allegiance to them, philosophers have set out to oppose not only the forms, but the everlasting *You* itself. To divine forms which have developed a momentum of their own and grown to be a focus of relation instead of the Formless and Imageless One they were meant to represent, philosophy has opposed the 'pure idea', sometimes even going so far as to envisage it as the negation of all metaphysical ideas.

It does not in itself entail the destruction of religion to make an abstraction of God. One who refuses to limit God to transcendence has a fuller concept of him than another who does so confine him. At the same time, the further an idea of God departs from anthropomorphism, the more it must be corroborated by concrete experience and completed by immediacy and nearness. For religion to be real, it is not imperative that the divine should be considered a Person, but we must be able to establish relation with it as our Vis-à-Vis—and not ours alone.

This has not happened. Yet the very repudiation of God by philosophy has stimulated religious minds to set out on a new encounter with him: and as they do so, they destroy the older divine forms which no longer do him justice.

In modern times, Buber ends, returning to the leading topic of relation and irrelation in *I and Thou* written thirty years earlier, irrelation predominates. In the pursuit of apparent security, prosperity and well-being, the world, our environment and the people who comprise it, even life itself, have come to be seen simply as possible sources of advantage and disadvantage to the self. The *it*-connection, swollen to gigantic proportions, has arrogated to itself almost uncontested mastery and command. The *I* of this connection is lord of the hour, an *I* that has all, makes all, succeeds in all, is incapable of saying *you*, of encountering another being. This all-powerful *I*-ness surrounded by *it* cannot by nature acknowledge either God or any true Absolute manifesting itself as of non-human origin. It steps in between and obstructs the light of heaven.[14]

But although we may seem to have done away with the world of transcendence and lost our earlier principles, and although our divine Vis-à-Vis may seem to have gone into eclipse, he still endures inviolate on the other side of the obstruction. Even if we rid ourselves of the very word 'God', he to whom it applies continues to live in the light of his eternity. He is not dead. It is we who are housed in darkness. The eclipse of God's light is not its extinction. 'Already by tomorrow, that which has interposed itself may have retreated.'[15]

As Buber's life drew to a close, with some deterioration in his health and increasing fatigue, honours and satisfactions of all kinds accumulated. He finished his work on the Bible. After Rosenzweig's death in 1929 he had continued with it on his own, planning once he had moved to Jerusalem to settle down to translating the very difficult book of Job, but for various reasons the work came to a halt. Then after the war, in 1948, the publisher Salman Schocken let him know that although there was no question of his taking the whole Bible, he would be glad to have Job when it was ready. Two years later another publishing firm, Jakob Hegner, with offices in Switzerland and Germany, made an even better offer for a new and revised edition of all the biblical books already published and for the remaining scriptural writings waiting to be completed. Buber was delighted. The five books of Moses were out by 1954, the historical books by 1955, the prophets by 1958. In the autumn of 1959, Job was finished and by the beginning of 1961 the work of translation was done. The final volume, the Hagiographa, saw the light of day in 1962. To his already immense corpus of writings, Buber could therefore add the rendering into German of the entire Hebrew Bible, partly in co-operation with Franz Rosenzweig, but mostly by himself: for even while Rosenzweig was alive, the actual work was largely Buber's, as his friend was the first to admit.

He also lived long enough to see the publication in three large volumes of his collected works by Kösel / Lambert Schneider in 1962, 1963 and 1964, with the supplement of another equally substantial tome devoted to his writings on Jews and Judaism published by Joseph Melzer also in 1963.

A further publishing event which must have afforded him much pleasure was the appearance in German of a volume in the series, The Library of Living Philosophers, edited by Paul Schilpp. Besides a short introductory section of his own 'Autobiographical Fragments', the book includes explanatory and critical essays on Buber's thought contributed by twenty-nine writers and scholars, among them Gabriel Marcel ('I and Thou'), Emmanuel Levinas ('Martin Buber and the Theory of Knowledge'), Emil Brunner ('Judaism and Christianity in Buber') and Robert Weltsch ('Buber's Political Philosophy'). In a third section given over to 'Replies to my Critics', Buber has the opportunity to answer objections and explain himself more fully wherever he feels he has been misunderstood.[16]

As for honours, in 1960 he was elected first President of the Israel Academy of Sciences and Humanities, and in 1961 to membership of the American Academy of the Arts and Sciences. Moreover, in 1963 he travelled to the Netherlands to collect the prestigious Erasmus Prize. On that occasion he gave an address, 'Believing Humanism',[17] which is couched in the same language that he had been using all his working life: that of relation, encounter and divine Presence, except that now he had to take into account the new threat to the world of technology and the splitting of the atom.

One last award went to Buber in 1964. He was given the Albert Schweitzer Medal for 'having exemplified the spirit of reverence for life and other tenets of the philosophy of Albert Schweitzer'.

No account of Buber's life and works can be complete

without some idea of what he thought of death. It seems therefore correct to end this brief enquiry with a short piece which, although he wrote it as long ago as 1927, must still have seemed valid to him in his old age since he included it in *Nachlese*.

> We know nothing about death, nothing but the one fact that we shall die. But what does it mean, to die? We do not know. It is therefore appropriate that we should accept it as the end of everything we can imagine. To wish to project our imagination beyond death, to anticipate in our minds what death alone can reveal to us in existence, appears to me to be disbelief disguised as belief. True belief says, I know nothing about death, but I know that God is eternity, and I know furthermore that he is my God. Whether what we know as time continues beyond our death becomes quite unimportant beside this knowledge that we are God's, who is not 'immortal' but eternal. Instead of imagining ourselves as being alive although dead, we desire to prepare ourselves for a real death, which is perhaps the end of time, but which, if this is so, is certainly the threshold of eternity.[18]

Buber died in Jerusalem on 13 June 1965 following a fall, aged eighty-seven. On his tombstone are written the words from his favourite psalm (73:23):

> *Nevertheless, I am with You always.*

NOTES

All quotations from the Bible are from the Revised Standard Version unless otherwise indicated.

Full bibliographical information will be found in the Select Bibliography, pp. 111–13.

Introduction

1 Quoted in Friedman, *Martin Buber's Life and Work*, Vol. III, p. 471.
2 Schilpp and Friedman, *The Philosophy of Martin Buber*, p. 690.
3 *Ekstatische Konfessionen*, Eugen Diederichs, Jena.
4 *The Philosophy of Martin Buber*, p. 693.
5 *Ibid.*, p. 718.
6 'Bekenntnis eines Schriftstellers', 'A Writer's confession of faith', runs the title of the introductory poem to *Nachlese*, a repository of excerpts chosen by Buber as being specially worth preserving.

1: *First Influences*

1 *Begegnung: Autobiographische Fragmente* 1960; *Meetings*, 1973.
2 *Briefwechsel aus sieben Jahrzehnten.*
3 *Briefwechsel* III, p. 293.
4 *Begegnung*, p. 6; *Meetings*, pp. 18–19.
5 *Begegnung*, p. 8; *Meetings*, p. 20.
6 *Begegnung*, p. 11; *Meetings*, p. 22.
7 *Begegnung*, p. 21; *Meetings*, p. 31.
8 *Begegnung*, p. 23; *Meetings*, p. 33.
9 *Briefwechsel* III, p. 290.
10 Translated into English by Paula Arnold in 1960 as *Old-New Land*.
11 *Briefwechsel* I, p. 199.
12 *Ibid.*, p. 200.
13 *Der Jude und sein Judentum*, pp. 755–782.
14 *Ibid.*, p. 783–794.
15 *Briefwechsel* I, p. 169.

[16] *Zeugen* = to beget, to procreate, but also to witness, to testify, so this is probably a pun. No similar significance is attached to *erzeugen*, to engender, the verb applied here to God.

[17] *Werke* III, pp. 967–8; *Hasidism and Modern Man*, p. 59.

2: *Encounter with Hasidism*

[1] Rivka Schatz-Uffenheimer, 'Man's Relation to God and World in Buber's Rendering of the Hasidic Teaching', in Schilpp and Friedman, *The Philosophy of Martin Buber*, pp. 403–34. See also Scholem, *The Messianic Idea in Judaism*, pp. 228–50. 'I am convinced that his selection corresponds as much as possible to the sense of his own message. I am not convinced that the sense of his message, as he formulated it, is that of Hasidism' (p. 249).

[2] *Major Trends in Jewish Mysticism*, Thames and Hudson, 1955, p. 260.

[3] See Gershom Scholem, *Kabbalah*, Keter, Jerusalem, 1974, p. 129; also *Encyclopaedia Judaica*, vol. 10, under the same heading.

[4] *Werke* III, p. 559; *Tales of the Hasidim: Later Masters*, p. 169.

[5] *Ibid.*, p. 390. *Tales . . . Early Masters*, p. 269.

[6] The Targums are ancient Aramaic paraphrases of the Bible.

[7] *Werke* III, p. 706; *Tales . . . Later Masters*, p. 309.

[8] *Ibid.*, p. 242; *Tales . . . Early Masters*, p. 124.

[9] Cf. G. Vermes, *Jesus the Jew*, S.C.M. Press, London 1983.

[10] *Werke* III, p. 84; *Tales . . . Early Masters*, p. 6.

[11] *Ibid.*, p. 287; *ibid.*, p. 169.

[12] *Ibid.*, p. 829; *Tales of Rabbi Nachman*, pp. 24–5.

[13] *Werke* III, p. 363; *Tales . . . Early Masters*, p. 243.

[14] *Ibid.*, p. 959–73; *Hasidism and Modern Man*, pp. 47–69.

[15] *Begegnung*, pp. 28–32; *Meetings*, pp. 38–41.

[16] *Werke* III, p. 973; 'My Way to Hasidism', *Hasidism and Modern Man*, The Philosophical Library, 1948, pp. 68–9.

3: *Early Writings*

[1] *Werke* III, p. 900; *The Tales of Rabbi Nachman*, p. 25.

[2] *Ibid.*, p. 903; *ibid.*, p. 31.

[3] Quoted by Scholem, *The Messianic Idea in Judaism*, p. 205.

[4] *Ibid.*, p. 209.

[5] *Werke* III, p. 185; *Tales of the Hasidim; Early Masters*, p. 69.

[6] *Ibid.*, p. 271; *Tales . . . Early Masters*, p. 147.

[7] *Ibid.*, p. 40; *Hasidism and Modern Man*, p. 112.

[8] *Ibid.*, p. 534; *Tales . . . Later Masters*, p. 146.

[9] *Ibid.*, p. 45; *Hasidism and Modern Man*, p. 121.

10 *Sanhedrin* 106b.

11 *Werke* III, p. 37; *ibid.*, pp. 106–7.

12 *Ibid.*, p. 38; *ibid.*, p. 108.

13 *Taanith* 2a.

14 *Werke* III, p. 558; *Tales . . . Later Masters*, p. 169.

15 *Ibid.*, pp. 28–9; *Hasidism and Modern Man*, pp. 88–9.

16 *Ibid.*, p. 165; *Tales . . . Early Masters*, p. 49.

17 *Ibid.*, p. 301; *ibid.*, p. 182.

18 Quoted in Louis Jacobs, *Hasidic Prayer*, Routledge and Kegan Paul, 1972, p. 123.

19 *Werke* III, p. 27; *Hasidism and Modern Man*, pp. 86–7.

20 *Ibid.*, p. 528; *Tales . . . Later Masters*, p. 137.

21 *Ibid.*, pp. 436–7; *Tales . . . Early Masters*, pp. 315–6.

22 *Ibid.*, p. 204; *ibid.*, p. 88.

23 *Ibid.*, p. 729; *Hasidism and Modern Man*, pp. 157–8.

24 *Ibid.*, p. 699; *Tales . . . Later Masters*, pp. 306–7.

25 *Ibid.*, p. 719; *Hasidism and Modern Man*, p. 138.

26 *Ibid.*, p. 721; *ibid.*, pp. 139–40.

27 The Czech author and composer. He settled in Israel in 1939.

28 *For the Sake of Heaven*, in which the postscript is however not included.

29 Hans Kohn, *Martin Buber: sein Werk und seine Zeit*, Melzer, Köln, 1961, p. 479.

30 *Werke* I, 1962, pp. 12–76; *Daniel: Dialogues on Realization*, Holt, Rinehart and Winston, New York, 1964.

31 *Werke* I, p. 14.

32 *Ibid.*, p. 45.

33 *Der Jude und sein Judentum*, p. 303; *On Judaism*, Schocken, New York, 1972, p. 57.

34 Franz Rosenzweig, *Briefe*, Schocken, 1935, no. 360.

35 Stenographisches Protokoll etc., XII Zionisten Kongress, Berlin, 1922, p. 715. Cited in Robert Weltsch's *Nachwort* to Hans Kohn's *Martin Buber; sein Werk und seine Zeit*, p. 435.

4: *I and Thou*

Quotations are translated directly from the original. References are accordingly to *Werke* I (1962), the first volume of Buber's collected works in German, and afterwards to the corresponding passage in the English translation of Ronald Gregor Smith, *I and Thou*, 2nd edn., 1958. For the sake of brevity, these are simply given as G (German) and E (English), followed by the page number.

1 *Briefwechsel* II, pp. 131–2.

2 'I and Thou' in Schilpp and Friedman, *The Philosophy of Martin*

Buber, p. 41.

3 *Buber on God and the Perfect Man*.

4 'Antwort' *Martin Buber* eds Schilpp and Friedman, p. 603 (my translation).

5 G. p. 85; E. p. 11.

6 *Ibid*.; *Ibid*.

7 G. p. 83; E. p. 11.

8 G. p. 85; E. p. 11.

9 See Peter Tompkins and Christopher Baird, *The Secret Life of Plants*, Allen Lane, London, 1974.

10 G. p. 83; E. p. 8.

11 G. pp. 87–8; E. p. 15.

12 G. P. 441 quoting *ibid*., p. 418; 'Man and his Image-Work' in *The Knowledge of Man* p. 165, quoting 'Distance and Relation', *ibid*., p. 66.

13 G. p. 105; E. p. 42.

14 Author of *De mystiek van ik en jij: een nieuwe vertaling van 'Ich und Du' van Martin Buber met inleiding en uitleg en een doordenking van het systeem dat fraan ten grondslag ligt*, Bijleveld, Utrecht, 1976.

15 G. p. 85; E. p. 11.

16 G. p. 96; E. p. 27.

17 G. p. 97; E. p. 28.

18 G. p. 106; E. p. 43.

19 G. p. 108; E. p. 45.

20 G. *ibid*.; E. p. 46.

21 G. *ibid*; E. *ibid*.

22 G. p. 111; E. p. 50.

23 G. p. 112; E. p. 51.

24 G. p. 118; E. p. 61.

25 G. p. 122; E. p. 65.

26 *Martin Buber: The Life of Dialogue*, Routledge and Kegan Paul, London, 1955, p. 58.

27 G. p. 128; E. p. 75.

28 G. p. 129; E. p. 77.

29 G. p. 131; E. p. 79.

30 G. p. 133; E. p. 82.

31 G. p. 138; E. p. 89.

32 G. p. 139; E. p. 91.

33 G. p. 142; E. p. 95.

34 G. *ibid*; E. *ibid*.

35 G. p. 149; E. p. 104.

36 G. p. 150; E. p. 106.

[37] G. p. 152; E. p. 109.
[38] Exodus was actually published in 1926.
[39] G. pp. 153–4; E. pp. 111–12.
[40] G. p. 159; E. p. 118.
[41] G. p. 159; E. pp. 118–19.
[42] G. p. 160; E. pp. 119–20.

5: *The Hebrew Bible*

[1] 'Zu einer neuen Verdeutschung der Schrift', Olten, 1954.
[2] *Martin Buber: sein Werk und seine Zeit*, p. 262.
[3] Rosenzweig, *Briefe*, Schocken, New York, 1935, no. 462.
[4] *Ibid.*, no. 508.
[5] *Briefwechsel* II, p. 242.
[6] *Der Gesalbte*, *Werke* II, pp. 727–845.
[7] *Briefwechsel* II, p. 442.
[8] *Ibid.*, p. 551.
[9] *Ibid.*
[10] In the *Nachwort* to Hans Kohn's *Martin Buber; sein Werk und seine Zeit*, p. 426.
[11] *Ibid.*
[12] Included in *Between Man and Man*.
[13] *Briefwechsel* II, pp. 625–6.

6: *In Palestine*

[1] *Briefwechsel* III, pp. 13–14.
[2] *Martin Buber's Life and Work*, Vol. I, p. 266.
[3] *Het Geloof van Israel*, H. Meulenhoff, Amsterdam.
[4] *The Prophetic Faith*, pp. 171–2.
[5] *Ibid.*, p. 195.
[6] *Ibid.*, pp. 195–6.
[7] *Ibid.*, p. 234.
[8] Meridian Books and The Jewish Publication Society of America, Philadelphia, 1945.
[9] Published first in Hebrew in 1943, and in English in *Between Man and Man*, 1947.
[10] *Between Man and Man*, p. 244.
[11] *Ibid.*, p. 247.
[12] Published in Hebrew in 1945, and in English in 1946.
[13] *Moses*, p. 8.
[14] *Ibid.*, pp. 82–3.
[15] *Ibid.*, p. 127.
[16] *Ibid.*, p. 169.

[17] Translated from the Hebrew essay 'On Betrayal', in Robert Weltsch's *Nachwort* to Hans Kohn's *Martin Buber: sein Werk und seine Zeit*, p. 439. For Buber, Jewish violence was a betrayal of Judaism and Zionism.

[18] East and West Library, 1973, p. 9; originally *Israel and Palestine*, 1952.

[19] Letter from Judah Magnes to Herbert H. Lehman in New York, 6 February 1948. In *Dissenter in Zion*, ed. Arthur A. Goren, Harvard University Press, 1982, p. 465.

[20] *Briefwechsel* III, pp. 133–5. Cf. also Paul Mendes-Flohr's introduction to *A Land of Two Peoples*.

7: *The Final Decades*

[1] *Briefwechsel* III, pp. 165–8.

[2] *Paths in Utopia*, 1958, p. 148.

[3] *Ibid.*, p. 7.

[4] *Ibid.*, p. 98.

[5] *Ibid.*, p. 149.

[6] *Briefwechsel* III, p. 317.

[7] *Martin Buber's Life and Work*, Vol. III, p. 241.

[8] In English in 1951.

[9] *Two Types of Faith*, p. 15.

[10] Gospel of John 20:24–9.

[11] *Two Types of Faith*, pp. 89–90.

[12] *Ibid.*, p. 131.

[13] *Ibid.*, pp. 162–3.

[14] *Eclipse of God*, pp. 166–7.

[15] *Ibid.*, p. 167.

[16] *Martin Buber. Philosophen des 20. Jahrhunderts*, W. Kohlhammer, 1963. The English edition of this book was published in 1967 as *The Philosophy of Martin Buber*.

[17] 'Gläubiger Humanismus', in *Nachlese*, p. 113.

[18] 'Nach dem Tod. 1927 Antwort auf eine Rundfrage', in *Nachlese*, p. 259.

SELECT BIBLIOGRAPHY

Works by Buber in German

Werke I, *Schriften zur Philosophie*, Kösel, München–Lambert Schneider, Heidelberg, 1962.
Werke II, *Schriften zur Bibel*, 1964.
Werke III, *Schriften zur Chassidismus*, 1963.
Der Jude und sein Judentum, Joseph Melzer, Köln, 1963.
Die fünf Bücher der Weisung, Lambert Schneider, Heidelberg, 1976.
Bücher der Geschichte, 1979.
Bücher der Kündung, 1979.
Die Schriftwerke, 1980.
Nachlese, Lambert Schneider, Heidelberg, 1965.
Begegnung: Autobiographische Fragmente, W. Kohlhammer, Stuttgart, 1960.
Briefwechsel aus sieben Jahrzehnten I–III, edited and introduced by Grete Schaeder. Lambert Schneider, Heidelberg, 1972, 1973, 1975.

Works by Buber in English

At the Turning: Three Addresses on Judaism, Farrar, Strauss and Young, New York, 1952.
Between Man and Man, Fontana, London, 1961. Transl. R. Gregor Smith. Comprises 'Dialogue', 1929, 'Education', 1928, 'The Question to the Single One', 1936, 'The Education of Character', 1939, and 'What is Man?' 1938.
Biblical Humanism, Macdonald, London, 1968. Ed. Nahum Glatzer.
Daniel: Dialogues on Realization, McGraw-Hill, New York, 1965. Trans. M. Friedman.
Eclipse of God, Gollancz, London, 1953. Transl. M. Friedman *et al*.
For the Sake of Heaven, Meridian Books, New York, 1958. Transl. L. Lewisohn.
Good and Evil, Charles Scribner's Sons, New York, 1953. Transl. R. Gregor Smith.
Hasidism, Philosophical Library, New York, 1948. Transl. C. and M. Witton-Davies.

Hasidism and Modern Man, Horizon Press, New York, 1958. Transl. M. Friedman.

I and Thou, Scribner, T. & T. Clark, New York, 2nd edn 1958. Transl. R. Gregor Smith.

I and Thou, Scribner, New York, T. & T. Clark, Edinburgh, 1970–1. Transl. W. Kaufmann.

Images of Good and Evil, Routledge and Kegan Paul, London, 1952.

Israel and the World: Essays in a Time of Crisis, Schocken, New York, 1963.

Kingship of God, Harper and Row, New York, Allen and Unwin, London, 1965. Transl. R. Scheimann.

The Knowledge of Man, Harper and Row, New York, Allen and Unwin, London, 1967. Transl. M. Friedman.

Meetings, Open Court Publishing, La Salle, Illinois, 1973. Transl. M. Friedman.

Moses, East and West Library–Harper Torchbooks, New York, 1946, 1958.

On Judaism, Schocken, New York, 1967. Ed. Nahum Glatzer. Transl. Eva Jospe.

On Zion: The History of an Idea, T. & T. Clark, Edinburgh, 1985. Transl. S. Goodman.

Paths in Utopia, Routledge and Kegan Paul, London; Beacon Press, Boston, 1949, 1958. Transl. R. F. Hull.

Pointing the Way, Harper Torchbooks, New York, 1963. Ed. and Transl. M. Friedman.

The Prophetic Faith, Macmillan–Harper Torchbooks, New York, 1960. Transl. C. Witton-Davies.

Tales of the Hasidim: Early Masters, Schocken, New York, 1947. Transl. O. Marx.

Tales of the Hasidim: Later Masters, Schocken, New York, 1948. Transl. O. Marx.

The Tales of Rabbi Nachman, Souvenir Press, London, 1974. Transl. M. Friedman.

Two Types of Faith, Routledge and Kegan Paul, London; Harper Torchbooks, New York, 1951, 1961. Transl. N. P. Goldhawk.

Books and Articles on Buber in English

Hans Urs von Balthasar, *Martin Buber and Christianity*, Harvill, London, 1961. Transl. A. Dru.

Arthur A. Cohen, *Martin Buber*, Bowes and Bowes, London, 1975.

Margot Cohn and Raphael Buber, *Martin Buber: A Bibliography of His Writings, 1897–1978*, The Magnes Press, Jerusalem, 1980.

Malcolm Diamond, *Martin Buber: Jewish Existentialist*, Oxford University Press, 1960.

——'Martin Buber: On Meeting God', in *Contemporary Philosophy and Religious Thought*, McGraw-Hill, New York, 1974.

Maurice Friedman, *Martin Buber: The Life of Dialogue*, Chicago University Press, 3rd edn rev., 1976.

——*Martin Buber's Life and Work*, Vols. I, II and III, E. P. Dutton, New York, 1983.

Haim Gordon and Jochanan Bloch (eds.), *Martin Buber: A Centenary Volume*, Ktav, for the Ben Gurion University of the Negev, 1984.

Will Herberg (ed.), *The Writings of Martin Buber*, Meridian Books, New York, 1965.

Aubrey Hodes, *Martin Buber: An Intimate Portrait*, Viking Press, New York, 1971 (= *Encounter with Martin Buber*, Allen Lane, London, 1972).

Rivka Horwitz, *Buber's Way to 'I and Thou'*, Phronesis 7, Lambert Schneider, Heidelberg, 1978.

Paul Mendes-Flohr (ed. with commentary), *A Land of Two Peoples: Martin Buber on Jews and Arabs*, Oxford University Press, New York, 1983.

Donald J. Moore, *Martin Buber: Prophet of Religious Secularism*, Jewish Publication Society of America, Philadelphia, 1974.

Roy Oliver, *The Wanderer and the Way: The Hebrew Tradition in the Writings of Martin Buber*, East and West Library, Cornell University Press, 1968.

Grete Schaeder, *The Hebrew Humanism of Martin Buber*, Wayne State University Press, 1973. Transl. N. J. Jacobs.

P. A. Schilpp and Maurice Friedman (eds.), *The Philosophy of Martin Buber*, Library of Living Philosophers, Vol. 12, Open Court, Cambridge University Press, 1967.

Gershom Scholem, 'Martin Buber's Interpretation of Hasidism', in *The Messianic Idea in Judaism*, Allen and Unwin, London; Schocken, New York, 1971.

——'Martin Buber's Conception of Judaism', in *On Jews and Judaism in Crisis*, Schocken, New York, 1976.

Pedro Sevilla, *God as Person in the Writings of Martin Buber*, Ateneo University Publications, Manila, 1970.

Paul Tillich, 'Martin Buber', in J. Bowden and J. Richmond (eds.), *A Reader in Contemporary Theology*, S.C.M. Press, London, 1967.

Pamela Vermes, *Buber on God and the Perfect Man*, Scholars Press, Atlanta, 1980.

——(ed. and transl.) 'The Buber-Lukàes Correspondence (1911–21), in *Leo Baeck Institute Yearbook* XXII.

——(ed. and transl.) 'The Buber-Schweitzer Correspondence', *Journal of Jewish Studies*, xxxvii, 2, 1986.

INDEX